SWING
MY WAY

SWING
MY WAY

LEE TREVINO

with Dick Aultman

ILLUSTRATIONS BY DOM LUPO

ANGUS
& ROBERTSON
PUBLISHERS

ANGUS & ROBERTSON PUBLISHERS

Unit 4, Eden Park, 31 Waterloo Road,
North Ryde, NSW, Australia 2113, and
16 Golden Square, London W1 R 4BN,
United Kingdom

First published in the USA
by Atheneum Publishers in 1976
First published in Australia
by Angus & Robertson Publishers in 1978
First published in the United Kingdom
by Angus & Robertson (UK) Ltd in 1978
This revised edition 1984
Reprinted 1984, 1985

Copyright © Lee Trevino and
Dick Aultman 1976

ISBN 0 207 14583 0

Printed in Shenzhen, China

To Ben Hogan

a great golfer who unknowingly influenced me to
   consistently fade the ball.

Lee Trevino

CONTENTS

Introduction: A New Way to Swing   3

1. Swinging Down Your Flight Path   14

2. Directing the Clubface   49

3. Finding Ball Level   83

4. Adding—and Controlling—Distance   100

5. Putting It All Together   114

6. Finessing from Trouble—and Elsewhere   124

7. Playing Around the Greens   144

8. Scoring with the Putter   155

9. Finding Clubs That Fit Your Swing   169

The Final Word   184

SWING
MY WAY

INTRODUCTION: A NEW WAY TO SWING

I GUESS THE ONE THING that makes golf so difficult for most people is that they never know for sure where the ball is going to go. Joe's been slicing his drives out to the right for five straight holes, so he aims his next one twenty yards to the left. Sure enough, he duck-hooks this one across two counties and the state line—a real John Dillinger.

The rest of the day Joe has no idea where to aim. Sometimes he guesses right· usually he doesn't. He comes in, pays off, drinks up, and heads home to grouse at his wife.

All of us are like Joe to some extent. I think that Jack Nicklaus is the greatest golfer in the world, but I know he'd be the first to admit that he *misses* most of his shots at least a little bit. So did Ben Hogan, Bobby Jones, and anyone else you can name. So does Lee Trevino; that's for sure. But we all succeeded at golf for one big reason: we all found a way to control our *bad* shots. I know if I hadn't done that I'd still be living on beans and beer. You'd still be thinking "Trevino" is Italian.

This book is about putting some consistency and predictability into your golf game. For the average player that means teeing it up on Saturday morning, after a week or so away from the course, and maybe after a few too many drinks on Friday night, and still having a pretty good idea where each shot is going to finish. It means knowing where to aim without carrying around a Ouija board.

In this book I'm going to tell you how to make a certain type of swing—my swing—because it's geared for consistency. I also believe it's the simplest swing around for most golfers to groove. I feel that Jack Nicklaus has a great golf swing, and so do Tom Weiskopf, Johnny Miller, and many others I compete against. I'm sure most would agree that their swings *look* better than mine. That's because their swings more or less fit a general pattern that the best golfers in the world have followed.

It's a pattern that looks good because it's similar to everything we've seen, read, and been told is correct about the golf swing over the years. This swing pattern has worked fine for Jack, Tom, and Johnny, who have each struck at least a million practice shots, but not so well for the masses who've tried to squeeze into the same mold—for the Joe's of the world who play for fun and end up being harassed, puzzled, and embarrassed.

There was a time when I played golf the way all the books and most of the teachers since Harry Vardon have said you're supposed to play. I had a "square" stance. I aimed at my target. I swung the club around my body, keeping my right elbow in tight, of course. And I tried to uncock my wrists at impact, not too early, not too late.

Well, I soon found out that they just didn't build courses big enough—at least, not *wide* enough—for my game. I covered more Texas real estate than Davy Crockett, Sam Houston, and L.B.J. put together. Every round was like a cattle drive.

Then one day I had a chance to watch Ben Hogan practice at the Shady Oaks Country Club in Fort Worth. I didn't have the guts to ask him any questions, so I just sat and watched him maneuver the

4

ball—high shots, low shots, draw shots, fades. He hit shots of every shape you could imagine, and they all finished so close together out there that his caddie could have been a blind man on crutches.

The thing I really watched as Hogan hit these shots was how he used his hips and legs. I remember getting a clear impression that he controlled his shots with his lower body. The more he led with his hips and legs, the more he'd fade the shot from left to right.

Well, I went back to Hardy Greenwood's driving range in Dallas, where I was selling buckets of balls, answering the phone, and giving lessons, and I worked and worked to find a way to control the ball with my body instead of my hands and wrists. It wasn't easy, but I loved every minute of it. I'd get up every morning about six and play eighteen holes at Tenison Park. Then I'd go home, take a shower, have a sandwich, and head for the range. I'd get there about noon so I could hit a couple hundred balls before I went on duty at two. Then for the rest of the afternoon and evening I'd hit balls off the grass in front of the mats, which were only about thirty feet from the pro shop. I could hop over to answer the phone or sell balls between shots. On a good day I'd hit a thousand balls, and I couldn't wait to get up the next morning and do it all over again.

This routine eventually led to divorce, but it sure taught me how to control a golf ball. I remember hitting wedge shots hour after hour toward the 100-yard sign out on the range. The sign was only about three feet high and five feet wide, but I swear I picked up a lot of quarters on the side by betting people I could hit it in one out of three shots.

Like I say, I developed a swing that isn't the prettiest thing you'll ever see, and it certainly isn't orthodox, but I think it's the most *functional* golf swing around. A few years ago *Golf Digest* magazine asked twenty-five professionals who they thought had the best swing on tour. Here are a few of their comments:

"Give me an action like Trevino's anytime. It may not look like poetry in motion, but it sure does work." —*Jack Nicklaus.*

"Trevino doesn't have a classic-looking swing, but it works. So it has to be one of the best." —*Gene Littler*.

"I guess you've got to go with the guys who are winning the most—Nicklaus and Trevino. Of the two actions, I'd pick Trevino's. Lee is the most consistent striker of the ball on tour. He's dead the same through the hitting area every time." —*Homero Blancas*.

"The best golf swing is the one that repeats most often. The swing that repeats most often on tour today is Lee Trevino's." —*George Archer*.

"What's your criterion? If it's repeatability, Trevino." —*David Graham*.

"Trevino doesn't look like much, but he has a fine swing because he does the same thing every time. That's the name of the game." —*Sam Snead*.

I apologize for bragging about my swing, but I feel I must because, in this book, I'm going to ask you to try my technique, and that means you're going to have to have some trust in what I say. I can't point to a lot of great golfers who've succeeded with a swing like mine. My swing *is* unique. In some ways it departs from everything that's been held sacred. But it works for me, and I'm convinced, absolutely without doubt, that it can work better than any other swing going for the vast majority of so-called "average" golfers.

I'm convinced of this because I am a teacher of golf as well as a player. Many people don't know it, but before I came out on tour I taught average golfers like you for seven years. I still teach at my club in El Paso and in clinics I give around the country. So I think I understand the problems of the learning golfer.

As a result of this teaching experience, I also know how easy it is for pupils to give up on something they are told to do when it doesn't work right away. For that reason I'm not going to ask you to accept everything in this book strictly on faith. I'll tell you what to do, but I'll also explain, with as much logic as this dirt-floor Mexican can muster, just *why* my advice is sound. Hopefully, this logic will help convince you that you can improve by using my method, whether you are big and strong, small and frail, or somewhere in between.

Yes, my golf swing is different, but that doesn't make it wrong. I really believe that the golf swing that's been taught for the last hundred years is old-fashioned. It's as out-of-date as knickers. It's a swing that worked fairly well generations ago, but it doesn't fit modern conditions.

For instance, our forefathers played golf in heavy wool jackets, dress shirts, and ties. They looked stylish and they kept fairly warm in the cold winds of Scotland. They played to unwatered greens where landing a downwind shot next to the flagstick was like trying to stop the ball on Interstate 95. Since they didn't have the machinery, or the inclination, to Caterpillar sand traps around all the greens, the best approach shot was a low runner that cut under the wind and bounced and rolled onto the dance floor. Golfers in those days needed backspin like chili needs sugar.

It's no wonder that those golfers, playing in such restrictive clothing, often with muscles stiffened by wind and cold, put their faith in the so-called "compact" swing. Right elbows were wedded to right sides. Hankies were inserted under the upper arm to see if the marriage was working; if one fluttered free during the backswing, it was a sure sign of divorce.

The best way to keep those hankies in place was to avoid any sideways sliding of the body. The hips were supposed to swivel to the right going back and to the left going through, just like "good old 'Arry Vardon" did it. Pupils were told to imagine swinging in a "barrel," never bumping against the "sides."

And "wrist action" was vital. With their arms encased in tweed and tight to the body, these players needed to throw the clubhead at the ball with their hands if they wanted to hit it past their shadows. With their hands they flicked the ball forward, low and running— just right for playing under the wind to those asphalt-like greens.

The end result was the best swing possible for the conditions,

7

but it was a swing that left very little margin for error. The hips were swiveling *around* on an arc; the arms were swinging *around* on an arc; the clubhead was traveling *around* on an arc. In short, everyone was trying to drive the ball straight forward, while moving everything on a curve. All the arcs had to be perfect for the clubhead to be swinging toward the target at the precise instant it reached the ball.

At the same time they were making all these arcs, golfers were cocking and uncocking their wrists in a mighty effort to get some clubhead speed. They were rolling the clubface open and then flipping it closed. And the more they rolled and the more they flipped, the less chance they had of making solid contact, even if all the arcs were O.K.

Today golf is an entirely different game. We play in light, soft clothing that gives with every move we make—even the sweaters and windbreakers we wear in cold weather. We play "target golf" to watered greens that hold like dart boards. We hit high approach shots that will carry over Robert Trent Jones's sand traps that often block out flagsticks. Golf has gone from a ground game to an aerial game. The more backspin, the better your control. Just fly the ball to where you want it to stop.

But golf instruction has not caught up with these changes. We're still trying to turn in barrels. People are still coming up and asking me, "When do you snap your wrists?" And some diehards are still wondering how Jack Nicklaus has won more major championships than anyone in history with his "flying right elbow." I'll bet you half of El Paso that Jack couldn't hold a *dozen* hankies under his right arm, and I'll bet you the other half he couldn't care less.

I don't mean to say that all golf teachers have failed to change with the times. Many have adjusted. The golf swing *is* slowly changing to fit modern conditions. You can see it more and more in the swings of the touring pros especially. But I still say we haven't gone far enough fast enough. And in this book I hope to be a bit revolutionary, by jumping you forward farther and faster than anyone has yet dared to do.

Mainly, in this book, I'm going to tell you how to make four things happen to your clubhead when it moves through the hitting area. First, I'll show you how to make it stay on the target line a little bit longer before it starts to arc back around your body. Second, I'll show you how to keep your clubface looking in the right direction a bit longer before it turns back to the left. Third, I'll explain how to keep your clubhead moving at ball level longer before it starts coming up in your follow-through. Fourth, I'll tell you how to control your clubhead's speed, so that you can do a better job of making shots travel the right distance.

These are the four things you need to make your shots more accurate, more consistent and more predictable, even when you're coming down that eighteenth fairway choking and leaking oil in a tight match. The longer you can keep your clubhead on line, at ball level, with the clubface looking in the right direction, the better your chances of making solid contact. You reduce your chances for error. You reduce the need to make a perfectly timed swing on every shot, and that's especially important if you can't fine-tune your game by playing or practicing every day. And you'll probably get some extra distance, first because you'll make solid contact on more of your shots; second because I'm going to stress the need for—and show you how to get—more acceleration; and third because I'm going to show you how to get some good out of those big muscles in your legs.

Now, to make all these things happen in your golf swing, obviously you'll need to make some changes. There won't be too many changes for most people, but they'll be big changes. The biggest will probably be in the way you set up to the ball and aim the clubface. If you can't, or won't, make this change, then I'm afraid I can't help you, because it's the biggest key to my method. The change in address position is what forces you—and also what *allows* you—to make most of the other changes. The new address position will change the way you take the clubhead back from the ball. It will allow you to use your feet, legs, and hips differently in your downswing—so that

FOUR WAYS TO HIT MORE SHOTS BETTER

In this book I explain four things that happen as I swing through the ball that can help you make better shots more often. The first thing that happens is shown immediately below: my clubhead is moving down my flight path for a slightly longer span (note larger arrows) than normal (smaller arrows). I talk about how I make this happen, and how you can too, in Chapter 1.

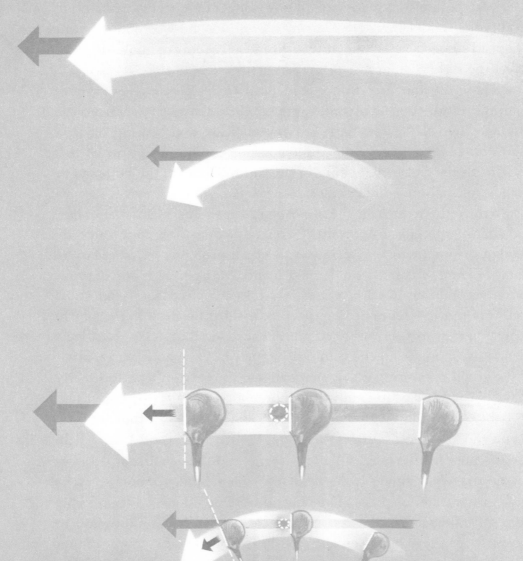

The second thing that happens as I swing through the ball is that my clubhead faces in the direction I want it to face for a slightly longer span (note larger clubheads) than normal (smaller clubheads). In Chapter 2 I explain how this makes more of my shots finish where I want them to finish, and how it can make yours do the same.

The third advantage of swinging my way is that the clubhead is more likely to move through impact more or less at ball level (note larger clubheads), so that the force given to the ball is moving directly forward instead of downward (smaller clubhead on left) or upward (smaller clubhead on right). I discuss how to make this happen in your swing in Chapter 3.

I talk about clubhead speed in Chapter 4, and explain why my type of swing is more likely to give me—and you—the right amount to make shots go the correct distance. Chapter 4 also discusses the other factors shown on these pages that help create proper distance, as well as increased accuracy, by making more solid contact more often.

you won't be swinging in the "barrel" any more. And it will allow you to let your arms swing freely *away* from your sides on your back-swing and, more importantly, through impact and beyond. You can save your hankies for nose blowing.

As I say, these changes are pretty drastic. You're going to look a little different and you're going to *feel* one heck of a lot different. In fact, what I'm really going to do is ask you to apply what my friend Dick Aultman calls the "brink of disaster" theory. This theory gets down to what I think has been wrong with the way golf has been played and taught all these years.

The problem has been, and still is, that we've set ourselves up to the ball and aimed the clubface and swung the club in a way that's supposed to give us our best chance of making a *perfect* shot. Well, this hasn't worked for most golfers because they seldom, if ever, make a *perfect swing*. Every time they're swinging they're reacting in a slightly different way than the time before. Because they try for a perfect shot, and because they make a different swing every time, they never know where the ball is going to go. One shot may be a slice to the right, the next a pull to the left, the third a pull-hook even farther left, and so it goes.

The "brink of disaster" theory forces you to react more or less the same way on every swing, and that takes much of the guesswork out of where your shot is going to go. The theory forces you to react one way time after time, because if you don't, you know you're going to be in real trouble.

I know this sounds scary, but I assure you that it works. It works because when you make a drastic change in, say, your address position, you know—you can really *feel*—what you must do to avoid disaster. And this makes you react the same way every time. You may not react to the same *degree* each time, but at least you won't roll your clubface closed on one shot and then turn it open on the next.

When we get into the actual instruction I'll be much more specific about this theory. I mention it here only to explain briefly why some fairly radical changes in your golf swing can actually lead to greater consistency.

Which leads me to the subject of practice. I've got to be honest and tell you that there is nothing magic about my method of swinging a golf club, or any other method. But if you've been shooting in the 90s for several years, perhaps it's time for a change. However, I can't promise to put you in the low 70s in a week, or a month, or even in a year. Learning golf is like learning a new language. It takes study, practice, and application.

You'll probably need to read this book more than once before it all sinks in, because I've an awful lot to say. But the more you study my words and practice what I suggest, the more you'll start to *feel* my message, and to play it better.

I also hope you'll look on learning to play my way as you would an investment in land. Don't sell out if it doesn't double in value overnight. Don't give up on my method if you should happen to dribble your shots along the ground for a couple of weeks. Something like that often happens when any golfer changes his or her swing.

Just bear in mind that you'll be substituting good habits for some bad ones you've no doubt been practicing for a long time. You'll gradually groove a new and better swing. The deeper you groove it, the more *consistently* better you'll play. That's what this book is all about.

1 SWINGING DOWN YOUR FLIGHT PATH

FOUR THINGS HAPPEN in my golf swing that make my good shots go pretty much where they're supposed to go, and keep my bad shots still playable. I'll tell you about the first of these four things in this chapter and the others in the next three. I hope you'll read closely with an open mind, because what I do might sound strange to you at first, especially if you've taken lessons or read a lot of golf books by other professionals.

The first thing about my swing that makes me more accurate more of the time is that I keep my clubhead moving down what we call the "flight path" a little bit longer than any other golfer I've ever seen swing. Keeping it on the flight path longer increases my chances of making my shots at least *start out* in the direction I have in mind.

Maybe you'll understand this better if you think about other sports you might have played. Take bowling, for instance.

The first thing a bowler decides is which pin he wants his ball to strike first, and where on that pin he wants it to hit. He's like the golfer who first picks out a target where he wants his shot to finish.

Next the bowler imagines how his ball should roll to this pin;

14

whether it should roll straight down the alley or curve in a certain way. The good golfer does the same thing when he imagines the flight of his shot before he chooses his club.

Next, the bowler picks the one spot on the alley in front of him that he knows his ball must roll over if he's going to hit the pin he's chosen with the shot he has in mind. The good golfer does the same thing when he checks his flight path and decides where his shot must start out.

Finally, the bowler tries to make sure his arm is swinging out toward this spot when he lets go of the ball. If he doesn't swing it out toward this spot, he won't execute the shot he's tried to make. Similarly, if the golfer doesn't have his clubhead moving down his initial flight path when the clubface reaches the ball, he can't make the shot he's planned.

It's the same with a baseball pitcher. If he's trying to throw a straight fast ball over the plate, then he's got to make his arm move toward the plate when he releases the pitch. If it's moving out to the left or right of the plate at that time, he'll probably walk a lot of batters. If he's trying to throw a curve ball, he'll try to swing his arm out toward one side of the plate and put some sidespin on the ball to bend it back into the strike zone. But he still must swing his arm along the initial flight path of the pitch he wants to make.

The point I'm trying to make for you is that, in golf, your shot will always start out in about the same direction your clubhead happens to be moving at the time it releases the ball. How many times have you tried to hit a straight shot that actually has flown on a straight line but several light-years left or right of the green? Well, that happened because your clubhead was moving on a flight path that was pointing a few degrees left or right of your target when the club-face impacted the ball.

Obviously you're not going to be a very consistent golfer if you can't make most of your shots at least start out where you want them to start. That means you've got to learn to control your clubhead's

YOUR CLUBHEAD'S PATH AFFECTS WHERE YOUR SHOTS START OUT

The direction in which your clubhead happens to be moving at the instant it lets go of the ball partly determines the direction in which your shot will start out. If the clubhead is moving directly down your intended flight path at that instant (top drawing), the ball will at least start out where you want it to start. If the clubhead is moving across your flight path and off to the left of it (middle drawing), the ball will start left of where you intended. It will start out to the right if the clubhead is moving across your flight path and to the right (bottom drawing).

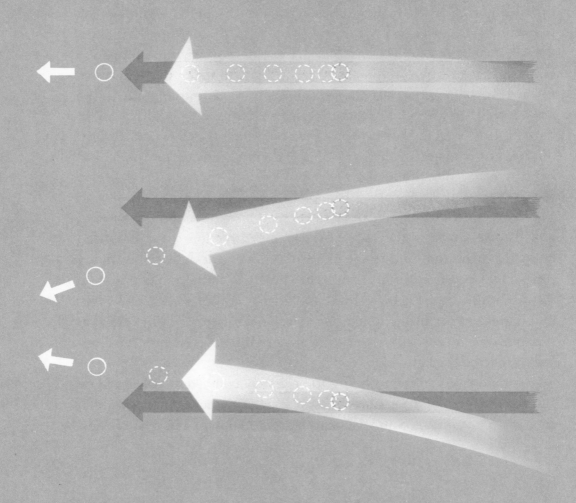

path through what we call the "impact area." That's the place where your clubhead is moving when it first meets the ball, then compresses it on the clubface, and, finally, releases it forward.

Keeping your clubhead moving down your flight path through this impact area would be as easy as boiling water if you could make your arms and the club swing back and forward like the pendulum on a clock. Then your clubhead would always be moving above and along your initial flight path throughout your entire swing. There would be no chance of its missing the runway or cutting across it laterally—left or right—during impact.

The thing about golf that makes the pendulum swing impossible is that you're always standing to the side of the ball. This makes your clubhead swing off your flight path on your backswing, because it *must* swing *around* your body. Then, if you make a good swing, the clubhead gradually comes back to coincide with your flight path on your downswing. Finally it moves back off that path and around your body again on your follow-through. So your clubhead is really moving along your flight path only for a very brief instant. If it doesn't catch the ball at that instant, your shot won't start out in the direction you had in mind.

Even good golfers can't keep the clubhead moving down the flight path very far—just a few inches at best. I think tall golfers have a better chance because they usually have to stand a little closer to the ball, which makes their swings more upright—more like the pendulum—but even very tall people swing on the flight path for only a very short span.

As I said, I've found a way to keep my clubhead moving down my initial path a little bit longer than everyone else, even though I'm built more like a jigger than a highball glass. My clubhead may move on this path only an inch or so farther than others', but that makes a tremendous difference. For one thing, it means I don't have to be quite so perfect about where I play the ball in my stance. I can play it an inch or so too far forward or too far back and still catch it with

CLUBHEAD SWINGS ON FLIGHT PATH ONLY AN INSTANT

If you could stand directly over the ball (smaller drawing) and thus swing a golf club like a pendulum, it would be possible to keep the clubhead moving directly over and along the initial flight path throughout the swing. However, because we must stand to the side of the ball, the clubhead must move around our bodies to some extent. Therefore, even in the best of swings, it can move directly down the initial flight path for only an instant before it returns inside—to the left of—that path during the follow-through.

the clubhead traveling on line. In short, I don't need to make a perfect swing every time because I've increased my margin against making an error.

I didn't make it through high school, but I do know that three is 50 percent more than two. If I can keep my clubhead moving on my flight path for three inches, and others can do it only for two inches, then I know I've got a 50 percent better chance of making my shots start out where I want them to start. I also know that, when I do mistime my swing a bit, I'm not going to start my shots as far off line as others do when they mistime theirs the same amount. The difference may be only an inch, but for me that inch has meant several hundred thousand dollars in my wife's pocket.

In this chapter I'm going to tell you how to lengthen the span where your clubhead is moving along your flight path through the impact area. To increase that span you will need to do four things. If you are now trying to play golf the way 99.9 percent of the teachers teach and other pros play, then one of these things you must do will be as different for you as walking on water.

First, however, I've got to give you a rough idea about where your clubhead must travel throughout your entire swing. There is no way you can make your clubhead stay on line longer through impact if it doesn't more or less follow a certain path during the rest of your swing. So let's talk about overall clubhead paths.

I've already told you that, because you're standing alongside the ball and turning your body, your clubhead must move off the flight path and around your body during your backswing and your follow-through.

You'd see what I mean if you were to take a piece of heavy paper or thin cardboard—a paper plate would be perfect—and cut out a football-shaped oval. If you actually want to do this, make your "football" about six inches from tip to tip, which is about the diameter of the flat, center portion of the paper plate. (You'll find it easier to get the right shape if you first fold the paper plate in half, then cut half a football out of that, and, finally, open it up to form the whole oval.)

Once you've got your football, cut it lengthwise in half, so you have two half-ovals.

Now, lay one of these halves down and imagine that it's big enough for you to stand on its straight edge and hit a golf ball that's sitting out on the middle of its curved rim, at the farthest point from the straight edge (see illustration).

If you were going to stand in that position and make a standard swing at the ball, your clubhead would more or less follow along and above the curved rim of the half-football. During the first half or so of your backswing, your clubhead would move back and around and up, along and above the curved rim to the right of where you're playing the ball. It would more or less retrace that same path during the last half of your downswing. Then, in your follow-through, it would move along and above the rim to the left of where the ball was.

This clubhead path I've described isn't really exact in every detail because I've deliberately oversimplified it a bit. But the outline of the half-football will give you at least an idea of the clubhead path that golfers have tried to swing along for centuries.

When you imagine your clubhead swinging around the rim of this half-football, you can see why it's been so difficult for golfers to start their shots in the right direction. Through impact the clubhead is still moving around the rim, which is curved. This means that the clubhead is moving down the flight path of the shot only a split second. If it doesn't contact the ball at that instant, the shot won't start off down the flight path.

The sort of clubhead path I've mentioned here works fairly well for skilled golfers who play and practice all the time, and neglect their wives and kids and jobs and everything else. Some of these players do develop the fine sense of timing and rhythm needed to make the clubhead catch the ball precisely when it's moving along the outermost part of the rim and down the flight path.

20

THE STANDARD RIM SWING

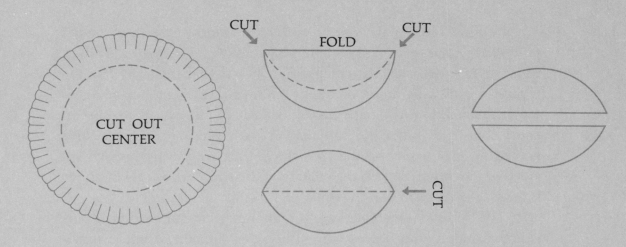

To help you understand clubhead path, both here and in later discussions, I'd like you to visualize a football cut in half lengthwise as shown above on the right. If you wish to actually make these half-footballs, I suggest you first cut the center portion out of a paper plate (above left drawing). Then fold that center in half and cut where indicated by the dashed line in the top center drawing. Finally, cut the "football" in half (dashed line in lower center drawing).

To imagine the clubhead path of the standard "rim swing" that has been taught to golfers over the years, visualize yourself standing on the straight edge of one of the half-footballs. You've positioned the ball on the outermost point of the football's curved edge—its rim. The part of the rim to the right of the ball more or less duplicates the path on which your clubhead would swing during the early part of your backswing and the late part of your downswing. The part of the rim to the left of the ball indicates its path during the early part of your follow-through. This image may not be precisely correct, but it serves to make the point that during the standard "rim swing," the clubhead path coincides with the flight path only momentarily. Most golfers do not have the ability to consistently catch the ball at that instant. Therefore their shots do not consistently start out in the direction intended.

But this traditional clubhead path hasn't worked worth a wooden peso for the masses of golfers who play once or twice a week, if that. Most golfers almost *never* catch a full shot at that instant when the clubhead is moving down the flight path. In fact, most golfers *never* move their clubhead *down* the flight path at all, except maybe on short shots and putts. I'd say that at least four out of every five golfers swing the clubhead *across* the flight path during impact. Instead of moving it back to the ball along the rim, they throw or shove it *outside*—out beyond—the rim.

The thing to remember here is that once your clubhead goes outside the rim on your downswing, it becomes difficult, if not impossible, to ever return it along that rim—along your flight path—through the ball. It must either stay outside the rim or be cutting back across again to the inside. If it stays outside the rim, obviously you'll catch the ball on the heel or shank of the club. If it's cutting back across the rim to the inside, it must be moving to the *left* of where you want your ball to start flying.

You'll see what I mean if you take your two half-footballs and put one directly on top of the other. Again, imagine that the curved rim you see is the path for your clubhead on a normal downswing and follow-through. Then turn the top half-football counterclockwise a few degrees. Imagine that your downswing is now going to follow this new rim. You'll see how the clubhead would move outside the old rim on the downswing, and then cut across the intended flight path and off to the left as it moved through the impact area and beyond.

If most of your bad shots do start out to the left of where you intend them to start, you are almost certainly swinging the clubhead back to the ball on a new rim that is outside the original backswing rim. The only other possibility would be that you're still swinging on the original rim but you're catching the ball too late. By that I mean you've positioned the ball too far to your left on the rim, so that the

WHY MOST GOLFERS NEVER SWING DOWN THE FLIGHT PATH

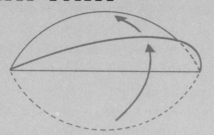 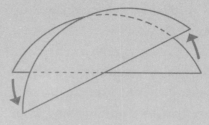

To visualize why most golfers never make the clubhead swing down their intended flight path, first imagine placing one of the two half-footballs directly on top of the other (top left drawing). Then rotate the half-football that's on top slightly counterclockwise (top right drawing). Now imagine that football's rim as representing your clubhead's path as it swings down to and beyond the ball. Obviously, its downswing path is now outside, or beyond, the original rim.

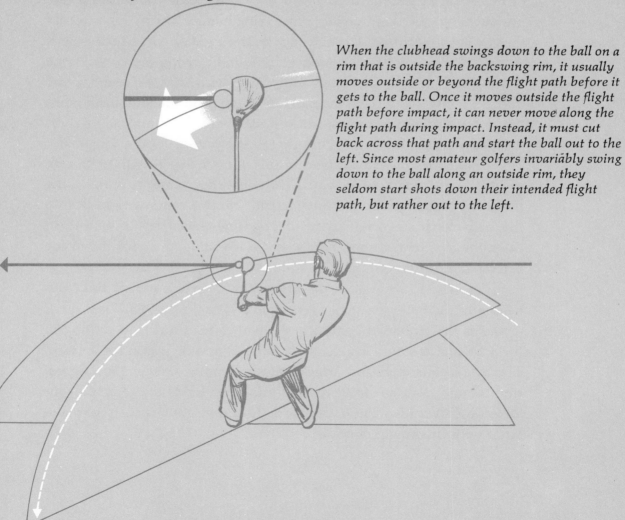

When the clubhead swings down to the ball on a rim that is outside the backswing rim, it usually moves outside or beyond the flight path before it gets to the ball. Once it moves outside the flight path before impact, it can never move along the flight path during impact. Instead, it must cut back across that path and start the ball out to the left. Since most amateur golfers invariably swing down to the ball along an outside rim, they seldom start shots down their intended flight path, but rather out to the left.

clubhead has started back around to your left by the time it reaches the ball.

Now, when you think about your shots, keep in mind that I'm talking here about where your shots *start out*, not where they finish. I don't care if your drives finish in the middle of the fairway, or even far to the right. If they *start out* to the left of target, you must be swinging your clubhead in that direction during impact. Chances are you're swinging it to the left of target because you've thrown or shoved it onto a new rim during your downswing that's outside the original. In fact, most golfers who slice their drives from left to right of target, and then pull their short iron shots to the left of the green, are swinging on this outside rim during their downswings. So are those whose shots start left and stay straight left or curve farther left.

Actually, most really good golfers don't swing along the same rim on both their backswings and downswings. Most swing along one rim going away from the ball, and then drop the club back a bit, onto a lower plane, as they start the downswing. This makes the club-head approach the ball on a rim that is slightly *inside* the original.

There are some advantages in this. One is that the slight change of rims to the inside gives you a little insurance against making the mistake of looping onto an outside rim. No one can swing back into the ball along the original rim every time—everyone is bound to catch the outside rim sooner or later. So it's safer to try for the inside rim on all normal shots.

Another advantage of the inside rim is that it moves the club-head into the ball on a shallower angle of attack. By this I mean that it makes the clubhead approach the ball like an airplane coming in for a normal landing, instead of one that's nosediving in for a crash. The more your clubhead attacks the ball from outside the original rim, the more it's got to be nosediving. That sends the force of your blow downward instead of forward. And *that* always costs you distance with the longer clubs.

So far I've been talking about the orthodox way of playing golf, which involves trying to swing the clubhead around a rim. As I say, this can work pretty well for skilled golfers who have a lot of time and desire to develop their talent. But it hasn't worked for most players. Swinging around a rim gives most golfers about the same chance of *consistently* starting shots on track as I do of becoming Miss America. Even the good golfers I know could be much more consistent if they could get that extra inch of clubhead movement down the flight path, but they'll never get it by swinging around a rim that is as curved as the one I've described.

So I say, let's forget about this "rim swing" that hasn't worked since Adam teed it up with Eve. Let's at least *try* a new approach.

I'd like you to again use your imagination with the half-footballs. If you actually cut them out, so much the better. Take the two halves you cut apart and put them down on a table with the straight edges again flush to each other, re-forming a football. Position this football so that the cut line runs across the table in front of you.

Now, slide the bottom half-football to your left and the top half-football to your right until the two straight edges are just barely touching. What you should have created is something that looks like a skinny figure 8 on its side, with the top half of the left-hand loop and the bottom half of the right-hand loop missing. The straight edges of the two half-footballs should now form one long straight line.

I'd like you to imagine that your golf ball is positioned in the middle of this straight line, where the two half-footballs barely touch. Imagine that the initial flight path for your shot is going to be down the straight edge of the half-football on the left.

Obviously, the best way to make sure this shot takes off on its intended flight path is to swing your clubhead down to the ball, and then beyond, by moving it along the straight edges of the two half-footballs. If you could make your forward swing follow these straight edges, obviously your clubhead would always be moving along your

A NEW WAY TO SWING DOWN THE FLIGHT PATH

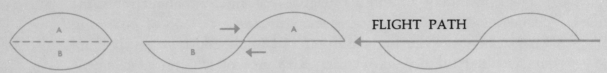

FLIGHT PATH

My clubhead stays on the flight path longer through impact because I do not think in terms of swinging it back to the ball around a rim. Instead, I try to make the "straight-edge" swing, which is contrasted with the standard rim swing on these pages. While it's impossible to duplicate the straight-edge swing as shown here in its extreme, the closer I can come to making it, the longer my clubhead moves through impact along my flight-path—even though that span may be only an extra inch or two. To visualize this swing, first imagine the two half-footballs positioned with their straight edges touching each other (top left drawing). Next, slide half-football "A" to the right and half-football "B" to the left (top center drawing). Finally, imagine that ball will be positioned at the point where the two half-footballs now barely touch, and that the target line runs along their straight edges.

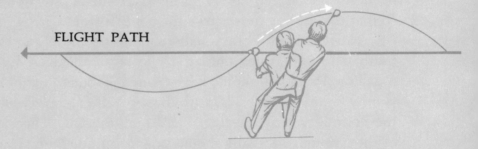

FLIGHT PATH

In the straight-edge swing, the clubhead must move outside the flight path at the start of the backswing. Golfers who attempt to do this from a square address position—feet, hips, and shoulders parallel to flight path—will probably find themselves toppling forward (top drawing). However, it does become possible to start the backswing to the outside of the flight path if you align your feet, hips, and shoulders angled well to the left of that path in an "open" address position (lower drawing). Remember that these drawings show an extreme version of my swing, to show only the potential of the straight-edge concept. My clubhead would actually move outside my flight path only an inch or two as it swings away from the ball.

FLIGHT PATH

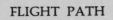

In the orthodox rim swing (top drawing), the club moves relatively far to the inside of the flight path. The golfer's shoulders and hips, when fully turned during the backswing, become aligned far to the right of target. In the straight-edge swing (lower drawing), the golfer sets the club much closer to his flight path at the top of his swing. His shoulders and hips, though fully coiled, do not align so far to the right of target.

FLIGHT PATH

FLIGHT PATH

The golfer making the orthodox rim swing (top drawing), cannot make his clubhead swing down his flight path for as long a span as can the golfer making the straight-edge swing. This is true because the rim-swing golfer's clubhead moved farther off the flight path during his backswing and his body turned farther to the right of target than the straight-edge swinger's, who returns his clubhead to the ball more from above the flight path than inside it. In other words, he swings down and through more on a straight line than around a rim.

FLIGHT PATH

flight path, just like a pendulum. It would never cross the runway, and thus your shots would always start out where you intended them to start.

I told you before that no one can swing like a pendulum, and that is certainly true. Thus it is impossible to swing directly along these straight edges. So the swing I'm going to describe to you isn't possible to *duplicate*. However, it will serve to show you a way of swinging that does make it possible for you to come *closer* to this pendulum movement than golfers have ever been able to swing before.

You may be wondering where your clubhead is to travel before and after it starts moving down this extremely long straight line. I'd like you to imagine that early in your backswing it still follows the curved rim of the half-football on your right, then follows the rim on your left late in your follow-through. Try to sense how it would feel to make this swing.

"It would feel terrible," you say? I agree. In the first place, early in your backswing you could never shove the clubhead far enough away from your body to make it start out along the rim on the right. Your arms aren't long enough. You'd fall forward onto your face.

The reason this backswing seems impossible to you is that you've probably imagined yourself addressing the ball like everyone has always said you're supposed to. By that I mean you've almost certainly tried to set yourself up "square" to your flight path: you've visualized yourself facing at a right angle to this path, with your feet, hips, and shoulders all aligned parallel to it.

But what if you changed your address position? What if you aligned yourself to the *left* by about 30 to 40 degrees? Try to imagine that. Turn yourself to the left by about one-half of a quarter turn.

Now, keeping the half-footballs as they are, again imagine swinging the clubhead back and around the rim of the half-football on the right. With the new alignment, to the left of your flight path, this backswing path should "feel" a lot more comfortable. You should be able to sense that now you could at least *start* the clubhead back along that right-hand rim during your takeaway, without having to shove the clubhead all that far away from your body. Actually, now that you've turned yourself around to the left at address, you could almost start the clubhead *straight* back, along the path of your new alignment, and still make it follow the rim of the football. You might have to let your right arm move out from your body a bit more than normal, but who cares? Remember Nicklaus's "flying right elbow"?

As you swing the club back, of course, you would still turn your body fully to the right, just as you've always done. This turning would make the clubhead continue its move around the rim of the half-football. But now there would be a big difference in where the clubhead moved *to* at the top of your backswing. The clubhead would move around your body and up, just as before, but it wouldn't move so far *inside* your flight path. In fact, at the top of your back-swing, your clubhead would have moved more or less *onto* your flight path.

Also, of course, you have now moved *yourself* into a new position. From the old orthodox "square" alignment at address, when you turned your hips and shoulders fully on your backswing, they went from being parallel to your target line at address to being aligned far to the right of your target at the top of the swing. If you tried to make a straight-line downswing from that old top-of-the-swing alignment, you'd shove the ball miles right of target.

But now, with this crazy new swing you're trying to imagine, because you've aligned well to the left at address, when you reach the top of the backswing your body is aligned much less to the right of target. You've made the same degree of turn as always, but now at the top you're aligned more parallel to your target—more to where you want the ball to go. In fact, if you set up to the ball aligned 45 degrees to the left, and then made a 45-degree hip turn going back, at the top of your swing your hips would actually be aligned exactly parallel to your flight path.

Now where do we go from here?

You'll recall that in the orthodox swing the clubhead more or less retraces the same path on the downswing that it made on the backswing. It returns back along the rim of the half-football to the flight path (and, hopefully, the ball for a brief instant), then continues to follow the rim back inside the flight path—to the left of it—on the follow-through.

Obviously, in this new swing I've asked you to imagine you wouldn't want to retrace your backswing path during your downswing. If you did, your clubhead would never swing toward your target—down your flight path—through impact, but would instead be cutting sharply across the line to the left. You'd then start all shots far out to the left of target, more or less in the direction you had aligned yourself at address.

Instead, why not imagine simply swinging the clubhead down the flight path and out toward the target? Why not swing down the straight edges of the half-footballs on both your downswing and beyond impact?

Again, this probably will seem impossible to do if you have learned golf the orthodox way. For one thing, you know your body must turn back to the left during your downswing: must reverse the turning that it made to the right during the backswing. Because you must turn to the left during the downswing, it becomes difficult to keep the clubhead moving straight down the flight path very far past impact. If you let your body turn to the left while your clubhead continued straight down the flight path, your left arm would have to leave your side.

O.K., so far I've described two types of swings. But I've told you that the first of them—the standard "rim swing"—hasn't worked for most golfers, chiefly because the clubhead moves around the rim instead of down the flight path. And I've admitted that the second—the "straight-edge swing"—is as far out as strawberry pizza, in that, although it keeps the clubhead on the flight path practically forever, to make it work you'd need to align yourself miles to the left at address and then practically disconnect your left arm from your body during your follow-through. By now you're probably ready to send this book back to Lee Trevino, C.O.D. But stay with me a little further.

What I've really been trying to do is open your mind to the fact that there just *might* be a different way to swing a golf club. Maybe we don't necessarily *have* to follow the old pattern. Maybe we don't *have* to set up to the ball with our alignment square to the target. Maybe we don't *have* to keep our right elbow in tight during our backswing, or our left elbow in tight on our follow-through. And maybe we don't *have* to turn our bodies around as though we were standing in a barrel.

The far-out swing I've described is definitely too extreme to be practical. I don't swing exactly that way, and neither should you. But then none of us really *needs* to swing our clubhead down the flight path forever, even if we could.

It is possible, and practical, however, to make a less extreme version of this "straight-edge swing." I do, and I think you can too.

I've already told you that one more inch of clubhead movement down the flight path is a factor that makes my shots more consistent than others, and it can do the same for you. And as we go along in this book I'll show you several other reasons why my swing—a less extreme version of the one I've just described—can make your shots more accurate, consistent, and even a little longer.

To enjoy my kind of extended clubhead movement down the flight path you'll need to make some changes, but these will cause some other nice things to happen. You'll find, for instance, that it becomes easier to square your clubface during impact, to make solid contact more often, to deliver the force of your blow forward instead of upward or extremely downward, and to increase your clubhead speed.

I told you that there would be four things you'd need to do to lengthen your clubhead's span of movement down the flight path. Now I'm going to tell you what they are. If you can practice and master these four things, you'll be able to make a less extreme version of the straight-edge swing I've just described. And then you'll also start to enjoy the other advantages I've mentioned above, and which I'll discuss in more detail later.

SET UP TO THE LEFT

If you've ever seen me play golf, you'll probably know that I set up to the ball differently from anyone else on tour. My setup differs from anything you've ever read or been told is correct. It's the one thing that makes me different from 99.9 percent of the golfers in the world. But it's also the one thing that I must do to make everything else about my swing fall into place. And you are going to have to set up more or less as I do if you want to have any chance of making your clubhead swing down your flight path that extra inch.

When I address the ball on a drive or long fairway shot, I'm aligned about 30 to 40 degrees to the *left* of my flight path. This means that lines across my feet, hips, and shoulders would extend 30 to 40 degrees to the left of the direction in which I want the ball to start. Thus, if I want to start a shot directly toward my target, I'm aligned that 30 to 40 degrees left of target. If I want to start a shot 10 degrees left of target and fade it back on target with a left-to-right curve, I'd actually align 40 to 50 degrees left of target—but, again, 30 to 40 degrees left of the initial flight path of the ball.

In a moment you'll see some of the reasons why I set up with such an extremely "open" alignment. Then later I'll go into more detail about my overall setup—ball position, posture, where to aim, and so on—on different types of shots. But right now I just want to give you the four main points of my method briefly and simply, so you'll get a clear overall picture of what we're trying to achieve.

STEP ONE: ALIGN YOURSELF TO THE LEFT

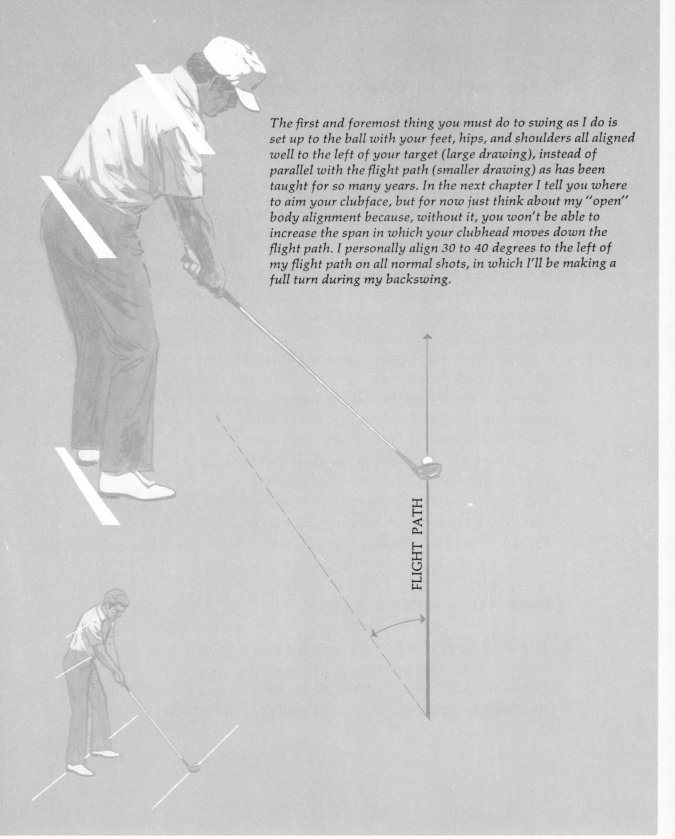

The first and foremost thing you must do to swing as I do is set up to the ball with your feet, hips, and shoulders all aligned well to the left of your target (large drawing), instead of parallel with the flight path (smaller drawing) as has been taught for so many years. In the next chapter I tell you where to aim your clubface, but for now just think about my "open" body alignment because, without it, you won't be able to increase the span in which your clubhead moves down the flight path. I personally align 30 to 40 degrees to the left of my flight path on all normal shots, in which I'll be making a full turn during my backswing.

FLIGHT PATH

START BACK OUTSIDE YOUR FLIGHT PATH

The second thing you must do in my system is swing the clubhead out beyond the flight path at the start of the backswing.

Remember the imaginary lines across your feet, hips, and shoulders, the lines that are extending some 30 to 40 degrees left of your flight path because of your open alignment? Well, start your clubhead moving back from the ball parallel to these lines, or even a little bit outside parallel. That will make it start back an inch or two outside your actual flight path. Then, as you turn your hips and shoulders fully in your backswing, gradually the clubhead will move back and up and around your body, just like on any other normal golf swing.

One reason I set up aligned to the left is that I want to start my clubhead back well *outside* my flight path, and that would be difficult to do if I set up to the ball in the conventional "square" address alignment. As I said, I'd have to shove the clubhead so far out away from me I'd probably fall on my face.

Above all, don't sweep the clubhead back quickly to the inside of your flight path—around your body—as you swing back from the ball. Start it straight back to the outside—extend your arms a bit—and then let it continue naturally up and around to your side of the flight path—to the "inside"—as you turn your body fully.

SLIDE YOUR HIPS AND LEGS

The third thing I do in my swing is make sure that my downswing starts with my hips and legs sliding laterally—sideways—to the left. I want this sliding to start before my wrists begin to uncock, or my shoulders begin to uncoil, or anything else happens.

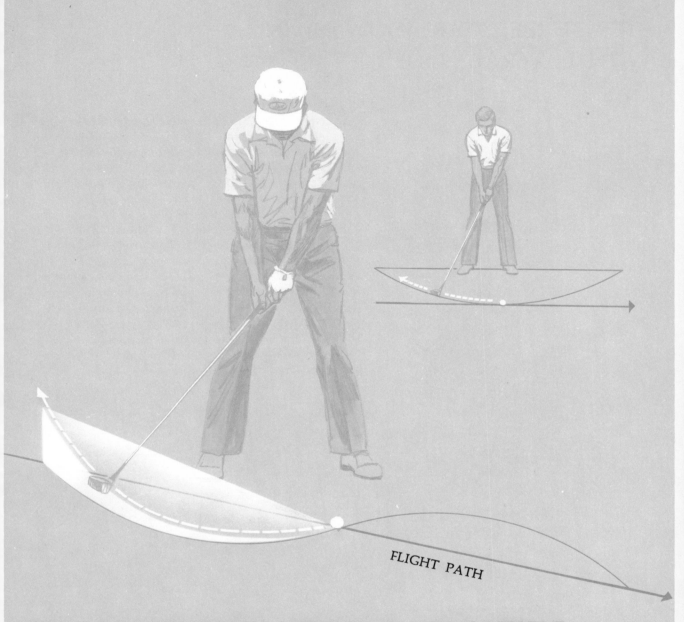

FLIGHT PATH

STEP TWO: START CLUBHEAD BACK OUTSIDE FLIGHT PATH

My takeaway differs from those who make the standard rim swing (smaller drawing) in that from the open alignment I showed you in Step One, you must start your clubhead moving away from the ball so that it moves slightly outside, or beyond, your flight path. I move mine a couple inches outside that path before it returns to the inside. Never let your clubhead swing back sharply to the inside from the open alignment. As your clubhead swings outside, then around and up, your shoulders and hips must turn fully and freely to your right as in any good golf backswing.

STEP THREE: START DOWNSWING WITH LATERAL SLIDE

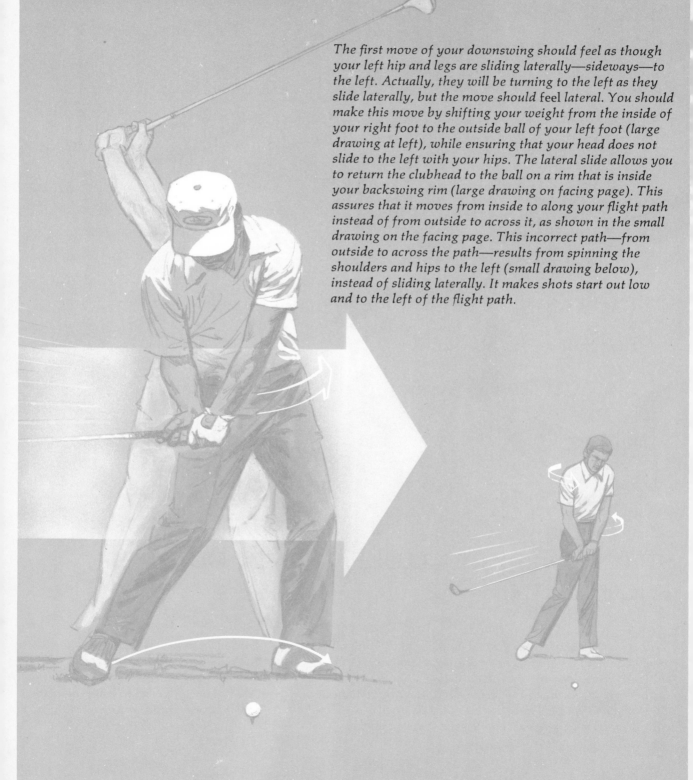

The first move of your downswing should feel as though your left hip and legs are sliding laterally—sideways—to the left. Actually, they will be turning to the left as they slide laterally, but the move should feel lateral. You should make this move by shifting your weight from the inside of your right foot to the outside ball of your left foot (large drawing at left), while ensuring that your head does not slide to the left with your hips. The lateral slide allows you to return the clubhead to the ball on a rim that is inside your backswing rim (large drawing on facing page). This assures that it moves from inside to along your flight path instead of from outside to across it, as shown in the small drawing on the facing page. This incorrect path—from outside to across the path—results from spinning the shoulders and hips to the left (small drawing below), instead of sliding laterally. It makes shots start out low and to the left of the flight path.

This lateral sliding of the lower body starting down is something almost all good golfers do to some degree, but I do it more than most. It's simply a shifting of weight from the inside of my right foot—a sort of pushing off—onto the outside ball of my left foot. What it should not be—and this is very important—is a shift of weight onto the left heel. That would make me spin my entire body around instead of sliding the lower body laterally.

This shifting must take place as the *first movement* of the downswing. Good golfers who are very supple even begin to make it while their arms are still moving back and up to the finish of the backswing.

I call this movement a "lateral sliding" of the hips and legs. Actually, it's a combination of sliding *and* turning. There has to be some turning of the left hip to the left, but you should slide your hips laterally *as* you turn. And you'll get the slide if your weight shifts onto the outside ball of the left foot.

Why do I stress this lateral sliding? Simply because it is this move above all that drops my club onto a good path for the downswing. What gets most golfers into trouble is the fact that it is practically impossible to swing the clubhead down to the ball along the exact same path that it followed during the backswing. It can be done, but it's as tough as boot leather to do every time, especially on full shots and especially under pressure. Almost all golfers swing the clubhead back and around and up on one rim and then down on another most of the time. Some even swing that way on putts.

I told you earlier that the poorer golfer usually throws or shoves his clubhead onto a downswing rim that is outside his backswing rim. I mentioned that this makes his clubhead, through impact, swing *across* the flight path instead of *along* it. It is this swinging down on the outside rim that makes so many right-handers' shots start out low and to the left. I also pointed out that the better player swings down to the ball on a rim that's slightly inside his backswing rim, which gives him insurance against looping the clubhead outside and across the flight path, plus a shallower clubhead path into the ball.

I believe that the inside rim is easier to control, once you learn how to find it in your downswing, and here's why: you can't *overloop* to the inside rim as much as you can to the outside rim because your body gets in the way of your arms—your body simply resists too much inward looping. But you can loop a tremendous amount to the outside, because when you throw your clubhead away from you there's nothing to stop it except the length of your arms.

Now, how do we get the clubhead swinging down on the inside rim? This is where the lateral sliding of the hips and legs becomes vitally important. When you slide laterally to the left as I do, the clubhead doesn't have a chance to loop onto the outside rim, because the lateral sliding forces the club to drop into a slot somewhere behind you. And this dropping the club into the slot is what starts it back to the ball along the inside rim.

Given my moves, you really don't need to worry about getting the club into the slot—don't need to consciously try to loop it to the inside and onto the new rim. It all takes place automatically if you shift your weight from the inside of your right foot to the outside of the ball of your left foot as I have described.

I did tell you that, while you're sliding your hips and legs laterally, they will also be turning to the left. The turning is the most natural part of this combination movement, because it's normal to unturn something that's already been turned. Since you turned to the right on your backswing, you'll have no trouble unturning to the left on your downswing—it's almost an instinctive reaction. However, the sliding to the left isn't all that natural, because you haven't slid to the right on your backswing (at least, I hope you haven't).

So most golfers get the turning to the left part of the movement O.K. They slam the left heel back down to the ground and shift their weight onto it, which gets them turning. The trouble is that this often gets them turning too much, because the more the weight goes onto the left heel, instead of onto the outside ball of the left foot, the more they'll turn, or spin, instead of slide.

39

The more you spin, the more you'll throw or shove your club-head onto the outside rim. And the more you slide, the more you'll work it into the slot and back on an inside rim. It's true that too much sliding, or too little turning, *can* bring your clubhead down too *far* from the inside and drive the ball out to the right of your flight path. But most golfers need more sliding and less turning, in order to work back to the ball on the inside rim.

The sliding will also help those players who can't get off their right side during the downswing, those who fall back onto the right foot. The proper lateral slide will force them to start the downswing with the hips and legs instead of the shoulders or hands, which is what causes the falling back in the first place.

Now let's tie the open alignment in with the proper takeaway and the proper sliding at the start of the downswing, since these are the three moves I've mentioned thus far.

First, the open alignment lets you start the clubhead back to the *outside* of your flight path on your takeaway. This takeaway path to the outside is important, because most golfers react in their down-swing to what they do during the takeaway. If you start the clubhead moving back on the outside of your flight path, you allow room for it to loop onto the inside rim during your downswing, which is where it should be. But if you swing the clubhead away from the ball sharply to the inside of your flight path, you run a high risk of leaving your-self insufficient room to drop the club into the slot on the inside. Instead, you'll probably react by throwing the clubhead to the outside, where you've left a vacuum for your arms and club to fill.

This, then, is why I set up aligned open to the left—so that I can start my clubhead back *outside* my flight path, and thereby leave room for it to loop onto an inside rim on my downswing.

There are some golfers who take the clubhead back outside the flight path, as I recommend, but then return it back to the ball on either the same outside path or on one that's even farther outside. Obviously this causes them to cut across the line during impact and get the same results (or worse) as someone who swung back inside the flight path and then looped to the outside. What these golfers lack is a full backswing turn and, then, the lower-body sliding action I've described.

The open alignment also puts you into a position at the top of your backswing that both *allows* you to slide laterally and *demands* that you slide laterally. I pointed out earlier that golfers who start out by aligning themselves "square" to their flight path at address eventually wind themselves up during the backswing, so that by the time they reach the top they've got themselves aligned far to the right of their flight path. Their hips might be aligned some 40 to 50 degrees to the right and their shoulders 90 degrees or more.

I think it's common sense that, the farther you're aligned to the right at the top of your backswing, the more you'll need to turn to the left on your downswing to make the clubhead swing through the ball toward your target. But the fact is that many golfers can't make this downswing turn. All they can do to avoid hitting shots to the right is to either throw the club back to the left with the hands and wrists, or shove it around to the left with the right shoulder. Both of these actions generally swing the clubhead outward onto the outside rim. Certainly these golfers cannot slide their hips laterally to the left early in the downswing, because any such sliding would leave the left side in the way, which would force the clubhead to drive the ball to the right, unless they could somehow flip the clubface closed to the left.

I'm all for people making a full backswing turn, and I can make as much backswing as anyone else. But, because I align more to the left at address, when I do turn fully my hips and shoulders are aligned closer to my actual flight path—less to the right of it—when I get to the top of my swing. Since I'm not turned so far to the right of my flight path, I don't need to make such a big effort of turning to the left on my downswing to get my clubhead moving back down the line. In other words, I don't need to shift my weight onto my left heel and risk spinning out, or to shove the club back around to the left with my hands and wrists. Instead, I can—and do—slide my legs and hips laterally to the left as I turn, by shifting my weight onto the *outside* ball of my left foot.

Finally, because I can slide freely down the line, I can also do a better job of dropping the club into the slot, which means that I can swing back to the ball on the inside rim time after time. In short, my clubhead is more likely to move *down* the flight path through impact, instead of across it from outside to inside.

I hope by now that you can see why it's easier for me to swing more down the straight edge of the two half-footballs that I had you lay end to end. I can swing my clubhead down the line longer in my downswing because, during my backswing, I've swung it more up above that line and not so far to the inside. And that is possible only from the open alignment at address, combined with the takeaway that goes somewhat outside the flight path starting back.

Now, there is one big danger in aligning yourself to the left as I do. Obviously, if you don't slide laterally and drop the club into the slot and swing it back on the inside rim—down your flight path— you're going to be in real trouble. If you loop the club onto an outside path coming down, so that it cuts across your flight path and off to the left through impact, your shots are really going to start out a mile left. In short, the more you align to the left, the more you put yourself on the "brink of disaster" if you don't make the lateral slide. So the lateral slide of the hips and legs—the shifting of the weight from the inside of the right foot to the outside ball of the left—is vital to my system—and to yours if you try it.

I'm sure there will be people who say they can't make this lateral slide with their hips and legs. Well, I really think any normal human being can make it with practice. Most people are probably on their feet at least an hour or two each day. The woman who keeps her house clean, cooks meals, and goes to the store probably gives her legs as much exercise in one day as I do mine during eighteen holes of golf. So does the youngster who plays outdoors with his friends after school, or the gas station attendant, or even the office worker who's always moving around from department to department and standing talking to others.

So making the lateral slide isn't a matter of strength for the vast majority of golfers, because our legs are the strongest parts of our bodies. It's really just a matter of learning to use the strength we've already got. It's a matter of training ourselves to do something in the golf swing that most people haven't learned how to do. It's a matter of using old muscles in a new way, and I think anyone can learn to do that.

You don't need to be on the golf course to learn this lateral sliding, or even to have a club in your hands. Just swing in your living room with an imaginary club until it becomes natural to shift your weight from your right foot to the outside ball of your left foot.

As you practice this lateral slide, you'll find that it's much easier to make if you give yourself *time* to make it. By that I mean you must not be in a hurry to get the clubhead back to the ball by rushing your backswing or starting down with your shoulders. Take it slow and easy so that your legs and hips have time to lead your downswing. The farther you try to hit the ball, the more you'll tend to fall back into your old habits of throwing the club with your hands or shoving it with your shoulders. Remember that your sliding hips and legs *must lead* your downswing if you're going to drop the club into the proper slot. And remember that you've got to give them training to slide and time to lead.

Also, as you practice this move, make darn sure your head and shoulders don't slide to the left with your hips as they turn and slide. Hold your head position steady. Try to feel as though your legs and hips are sliding out from underneath your shoulders.

43

SWING THROUGH THE BALL AND OUT

The fourth and final thing I do in my swing to keep the clubhead moving down the flight path for a longer span is to let my left arm move away from my side and down that path as I swing past impact.

As I've said before, whichever way you make a golf swing you must let the clubhead swing off the flight path—back around the body to the left—sooner or later after impact. This has to happen simply because we're standing off to the side of the ball. Even with my lateral slide, my clubhead would move quickly back to the left after impact if I didn't let my left arm leave my side. I don't mean that it comes loose at the shoulder, but simply that it continues to swing forward, staying on the same path I've been swinging it along through impact. This extension is something the old-timers playing in their tweed coats and dress shirts couldn't make without swaying their heads and shoulders and everything else to the left.

Naturally, the longer I keep swinging my left arm on this path past impact, the longer my clubhead is going to keep moving down the flight path before it starts coming back around to the left. It's got to swing to the left sooner or later, but if I can make that happen later—even just an inch later—then I've got a much better chance of starting my shots out on the flight path I've chosen.

You may have noticed if you've watched me play that, during my downswing and early follow-through, my right shoulder makes a very "deep" swing under my chin. I swing my right shoulder deeper than most good golfers—and almost all poor golfers—because of my lateral slide on the downswing and my left-arm extension down the flight path past impact. If I didn't slide my hips and extend that arm—or if I didn't hold my head in one position the whole time—the right shoulder wouldn't work "under" so much. Instead, it would turn more horizontally—like a merry-go-round—during my downswing.

44

STEP FOUR: LET LEFT ARM LEAVE YOUR SIDE

To keep your clubhead moving down your flight path a little longer
past impact, you must let your left arm leave your left side as you
swing through the ball (large drawing). When this happens
correctly you'll feel your right shoulder working under (large
drawing) instead of around (small drawing). The extent that the
clubhead can stay on the flight path past impact is exaggerated in
the large drawing, but even a fraction of an inch more extension of
on-path movement will improve your chances for starting shots
in the direction you intend.

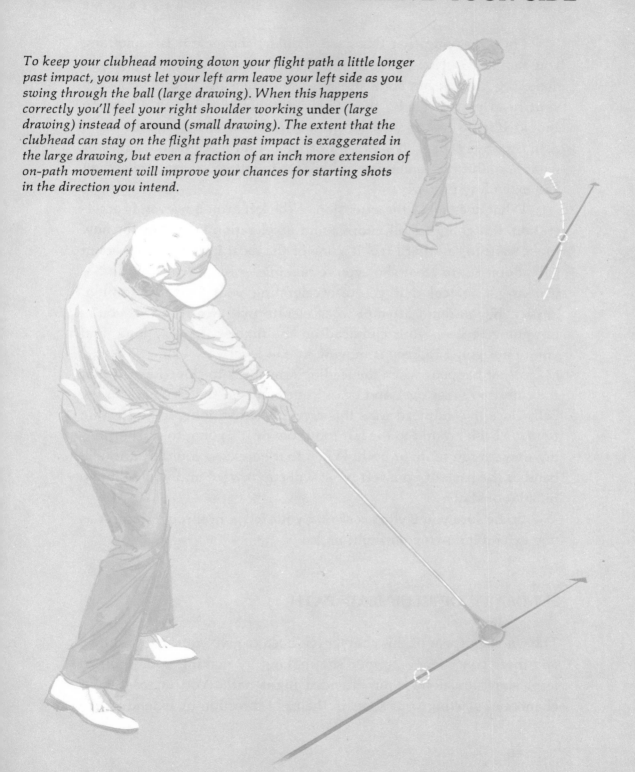

I'm not saying that this deep shoulder movement is something you should consciously try to do. What I *am* saying is that, if you make my kind of hip slide and left-arm extension, and if you keep your head pretty steady, then this deep shoulder turn is what you should start to *feel* as your left arm swings out and down the flight path. In other words, it's a *result* of what I do more than a *cause* of what I do. But it's something to look for to tell you if you are sliding and extending properly.

What does *cause* the extension of the left arm, however, is acceleration. I'm going to talk more about acceleration later, but for now I just want to say that I feel it's one of the most important factors in golf. I don't care what shot you're making—even a two-foot putt— you've *got* to feel that you're accelerating your left arm through impact. If you don't attempt to accelerate that arm forward, you're not going to keep your clubhead on the flight path very long, and you're not going to keep it moving at ball level very long.

What happens when the leading arm starts to slow down is that the clubhead takes over and beats your hands in the race back to the ball. Once the clubhead wins this race, it's either going to be starting to move back around to the left too soon, or it's going to start swinging upward too soon, or both. When that happens, your left arm will bend or the back of your left wrist will cup inward and you will mis-hit a lot of shots.

So be sure you try to *accelerate* your left arm through impact as you extend it down your flight path.

SUMMARY OF CLUBHEAD PATH

The whole purpose of this chapter has been to give you more accuracy and more consistency in your shotmaking by making your shots at least start out along your intended flight path. You increase your chances of starting your shots in the right direction by extending the span that your clubhead moves down your flight path through the impact area.

To show you how to extend this span of clubhead movement down the flight path, I've described two types of swing: (1) the standard swing around the rim of a half-football and (2) an extremely different swing, first around the rim of one half-football and then down the straight edges of two half-footballs.

The characteristics of these two swings are as follows:

THE "RIM SWING"

1. Stance and body alignment "square" at address.
2. Clubhead movement off the flight path to the inside early in the backswing.
3. Body alignment far to the right of target at the top of backswing.
4. Clubhead set far inside the flight path at top of backswing.
5. Need for full turning to left on downswing, returning weight onto left heel.
6. Little chance for lateral sliding to left on downswing.
7. High potential for throwing or shoving clubhead onto an outside rim during downswing.
8. High potential for swinging clubhead from outside the flight path to inside during impact.
9. High potential for chopping downward into ball.
10. Need for precise timing and rhythm during downswing to return clubhead along the rim.
11. Need for precise timing and ball positioning to make impact coincide with the brief instant when clubhead swings down the flight path.
12. Early clubhead return to inside of the flight path during, or just after, impact.

THE "STRAIGHT-EDGE SWING"

1. Body and stance alignment 30 to 40 degrees to left of the flight path at address.

2. Clubhead movement outside the flight path during takeaway, then around to the inside as hips and shoulders turn fully during backswing.

3. Body alignment less to right of target at top of backswing, closer to parallel with the flight path.

4. Clubhead set less inside the flight path at top of backswing.

5. Less need for full turning to left on downswing.

6. More chance for lateral sliding to left on downswing, shifting weight from inside of right foot onto outside ball of left foot.

7. Less chance of throwing or shoving clubhead to the outside during downswing, because lateral sliding drops club into slot on inside rim.

8. Increased potential for swinging clubhead down the flight path instead of across it from outside to inside.

9. Less potential for chopping down to ball, since club has been looped to inside instead of outside.

10. Less need for precise timing and rhythm because clubhead moves down the flight path for longer span.

11. Greater need for left-arm extension down the flight path beyond impact demands, and creates, greater forward acceleration.

I think you now can see why I favor my modified version of the extreme "straight-edge swing" I've described in this chapter. But remember that the *only* way to make this swing is to set up aligned to the left. That's what allows you to make the proper takeaway outside the flight path. It's what allows you to make the lateral slide. And it's what demands that you swing out along your flight path after impact. Without the open alignment to the left, you'll never get that extra inch or so of clubhead movement down the flight path.

2 DIRECTING THE CLUBFACE

A<small>T THE START</small> of the last chapter I promised to tell you the four things I achieve with my golf swing that give me an edge when it comes to hitting shots where I want them to go. Then I explained the first thing I achieve—a longer span of clubhead movement down the flight path through impact, which improves my chances of making my shots at least *start out* in the right direction.

In this chapter we'll talk in detail about the second thing I achieve with my swing that keeps me on target, or close to target, on most of my shots. This second achievement has to do with what happens to shots *after* they've started out in the right direction. It's what gives me an edge when it comes to making my shots curve in flight the way I want them to curve.

When I say I want my shots to curve, I mean just that. And before I tell you how I make my shots curve as I've planned, I'd better convince you that you'll never be a consistent, accurate golfer if you're now trying to hit every shot straight.

I know that for many of you the idea of curving shots might make as much sense as walking backwards, especially if keeping golf balls on the course is already your big problem. The truth is that hitting shots that curve is a problem of accuracy only if you don't know beforehand which *way* they're going to curve and have a pretty good idea of how *big* the curve will be. And I suspect that, if you don't know now what kind of curve to expect on a given shot, one reason might just be that you're trying to hit all your shots dead straight.

What you need to understand is that the toughest shot to make in golf is the straight shot. Ask Palmer, Nicklaus, Player, Miller, or anyone else who ever won a U.S. Open. Anytime you put those gentlemen more than 175 yards away from the flagstick, I'll bet you all the chips in Vegas that the last thing they are trying to do is hit a straight shot. They're trying to fade that shot in from the left side or draw it in from the right.

The reason the straight shot is so tough to make consistently is simple to explain. Let's say you've got a 200-yard hole and that's about how far you hit your good drives. Now, to make that drive fly perfectly straight, you've got to hit the ball so that it carries practically no sidespin, because it's the sidespin that makes a shot curve sideways.

To hit a drive with no sidespin, you've got to swing the club in such a way that at the instant of impact its face is *looking* in exactly the same direction as it is *moving*. Think about that for a minute, because it's important. To make a drive go dead straight to your target, you've got to: (1) have your clubhead moving *toward* the target when it lets go of the ball, and (2) you've got to have your clubface looking directly *at* the target. Now, if you think it isn't difficult to achieve both of those things when your clubhead's out there about three feet away from your hands and moving at around a hundred miles an hour, then I'll guarantee you don't need this book. What you need is a dime to call me collect so I can sponsor you on the P.G.A. tour.

The point is that no human being can be *that* perfect time after

50

time. Sure, you can play for shots to go straight at your target every time, but it's not going to happen very often. On most of your long shots you might get your clubhead moving on target, but your club-face will be looking at least a degree or two to the left or right. Or you'll get your clubface looking at your target, but your clubhead will be moving a degree or two to the left or right. Whatever the misalign-ment, anytime your clubhead is facing in a different direction from where it's moving, you're going to get some sidespin, and therefore some curve on your long shots.

Now, it is possible to hit short shots fairly straight, even with some sidespin. This is because on shots with highly lofted clubs—wedges, 7, 8, and 9 irons—you get more backspin on the ball, which will often keep the ball on line by overpowering any sidespin it may be carrying. But you can't get all that much backspin on your longer shots with the woods and less lofted irons, and that's when sidespin takes over and the ball curves sideways. In fact, that's why the drive, played with the least lofted club, is the most difficult shot for most people to hit straight.

Good golfers have played the game long enough to know that they aren't good enough to hit long shots straight very often. They also know that, if they do try to hit a straight shot, and then it does curve on them, it's certain to curve *away* from where they want it to go—away from the target where they aimed in the first place. Also, because they can never know which way it's going to curve, they never know if they're going to miss left or right of target.

So what the good golfer does is plan beforehand the direction in which he's going to make each shot curve. He aims himself and his club at address so that the ball's initial flight path will be to the left or right of target. And then he plays the shot that will make it curve back *toward* the target.

By playing for a curved shot, the good golfer knows pretty much which way the ball is going to curve, which means that he can only miss it in one direction. Also, he knows that if he doesn't curve

BEND YOUR LONG SHOTS FOR BETTER CONSISTENCY

To make long shots fly straight time after time takes more precise skill than even expert golfers possess. Therefore, assuming that most shots will curve either right or left, it does not pay to play for a straight shot with wood clubs or the longer-shafted irons. The drawing at right shows that if you play for a straight shot (dashed line), and then curve it in either direction (solid lines), the ball will always fly, bounce, and roll away from the target.

The smart golfer plays his woods and long irons to curve in a given direction, either from right to left or, as shown here, from left to right. Then, if the ball doesn't curve as much as expected (solid arrow on the right), it still will curve, bounce and roll toward the target. If it curves more than expected (solid arrow on the left), it still won't miss the target by as much as it would have if the player had not anticipated any curve in that direction. In this chapter I explain how to adjust your set-up alignment and clubface aim to play for shots that curve slightly. Experts can curve shots at will in either direction. Less skillful players should, at first, learn to master the art of curving shots in one direction only.

it as much as he'd expected, the ball is still going to be bouncing and rolling *toward* his target. If he curves it more than he'd expected to, at least it's not going to finish as far off target as it would have if he hadn't originally allowed for some curving.

Again, it's like bowling. The good bowler knows he's not good enough to roll a straight ball every time; that to roll a straight ball he's got to be swinging his arm straight toward his target, with his palm facing in exactly that same direction as he lets go of the ball. If his palm is facing left or right of his "flight path," where he's trying to swing his arm, the ball is going to curve left or right. And he knows if he tries for a straight roll every time, one time his palm might be facing left and the next time right.

So the bowler adds some predictability to his game by making the ball curve in a given direction whenever the situation allows. Generally, the right-handed bowler swings his arm down an "initial flight path" that is to the right of his target, then releases the ball with his palm facing slightly to the left of that path. Just as in golf, when the clubface is looking to the left of where the clubhead is moving, the shot is going to be curved to the left by sidespin.

Thus the bowler, in preplanning his curve, knows the ball will be bending away from the alley and toward the pins, instead of away from the pins and toward the alley. Similarly, the good golfer bends his shots away from trouble and toward his target.

Now, while I think any golfer should work on playing his long shots to curve into the target, normally I don't think he'd want a whole lot of curve. The reason is that too much curve takes away from your distance. To curve a shot you need some sidespin, and to get sidespin you need a glancing blow with the clubhead. When the blow becomes too glancing, you don't get enough clubhead force moving directly into the back of the ball to project it solidly forward.

So in this chapter I'm going to tell you how to learn to control the *direction* in which your shots curve, and how to control the *amount* they curve. Once you learn this lesson, you'll know where to aim to make the shot you want to make, which is what accuracy in golf is all about. And the one thing I won't tell you to do is to aim *at* your target.

From all this, you will undoubtedly have guessed what the second thing is that I achieve in my golf swing that gives me my accuracy. Not only do I keep my clubhead moving down the flight path for a longer span, but I also *keep my clubface looking where I want it to look for a longer time through the impact area* than do most golfers.

Remember, it's the facing of the club when it lets go of the ball that determines how your shot will curve in flight. The longer you can keep that clubface looking where it's supposed to be looking, the better your chances are of making each shot curve the way you want it to curve.

There wouldn't be any problem in controlling the club's facing during the swing if we could keep it looking in the same direction the whole time. Unfortunately, it's just as impossible to keep your clubface looking in the same direction throughout your swing as it is to make your clubhead swing along your flight path indefinitely, and for the same reason—because you're standing off to the side of the ball.

Generally speaking, the path your clubhead swings along has a lot to do with where the clubface is going to be looking. Unless you do some fancy manipulation with your hands and wrists and arms, your clubface will tend to look *down* the path the clubhead is moving *along*. That means that if you make the standard rim swing, where your clubhead is moving down the flight path for only an instant in the impact area, then your clubface will probably be looking where you want it to look for only an instant. However, if you make a swing like mine, where the clubhead is moving down the flight path a bit longer in the impact area, then your clubface is also going to be looking where you want it to look for a little bit longer.

To see what I mean, extend your left arm out in front of you,

54

BALL WILL CURVE WHERE CLUBFACE IS LOOKING

To a certain extent, the direction in which the clubface happens to be looking when the ball leaves it determines the direction in which it will curve in flight. If it's looking to the right of the path on which it is moving (top drawing), the ball will start out more or less on that path and then curve to the right. If the clubface looks in the same direction as it is moving (middle drawing), the ball will fly straight in whatever direction that path of movement happens to be. If the clubface looks left of its path of movement (bottom drawing), the ball will eventually curve to the left of that path.

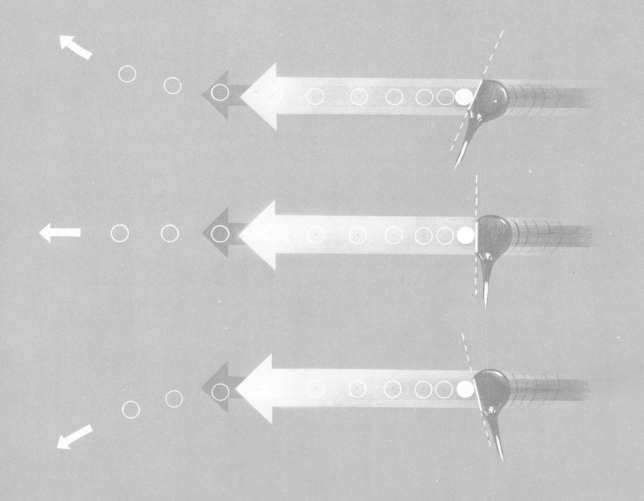

keeping your fingers together but holding your palm open. Imagine that the back of this hand is your clubface.

Now make the rim swing around the half-football. Start with your hand facing down your flight path. Make your hand follow around the right half of the rim on your backswing, return along this rim on your downswing, and then follow around the left half of the rim on your follow-through. See how the back of your hand faces toward your "target" for only an instant before it turns off to the left as you follow through.

Now use this same hand to make the straight-edge swing. Remember to align to the left of your flight path, but this time also face the back of your hand to the *left* of your flight path, in the same direction that you are aligned. Remember to swing your hand *outside* your flight path on your takeaway. Remember to slide your legs and hips laterally to the left as you turn in your downswing. And remember to swing your hand down and out along your flight path throughout your forward swing.

When you make this swing, you'll see that the back of your left hand—your imaginary clubface—continues to look down your flight path throughout much of your downswing and well into your follow-through. This should give you an idea of how my swing keeps the clubface looking where I want it to look for a longer span through the impact area.

As you made these two types of swings with your left arm and hand, you should have felt a difference in the way they reacted. When you made the rim swing, your hand and arm should have felt like a swinging door that was opening on your backswing and closing on your downswing and follow-through. Try the rim swing again until you get this feeling.

Now try the straight-edge swing again. Your hand and arm should feel different as they swing down and out along the flight path on your forward swing. You no longer should feel that the door is closing, but rather a resistance to this closing.

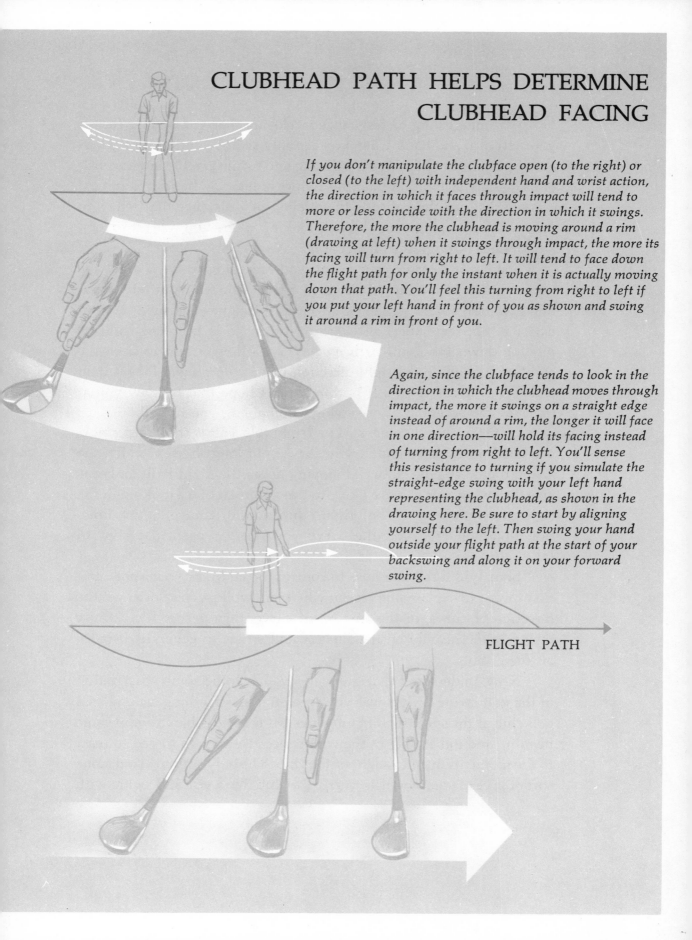

CLUBHEAD PATH HELPS DETERMINE CLUBHEAD FACING

If you don't manipulate the clubface open (to the right) or closed (to the left) with independent hand and wrist action, the direction in which it faces through impact will tend to more or less coincide with the direction in which it swings. Therefore, the more the clubhead is moving around a rim (drawing at left) when it swings through impact, the more its facing will turn from right to left. It will tend to face down the flight path for only the instant when it is actually moving down that path. You'll feel this turning from right to left if you put your left hand in front of you as shown and swing it around a rim in front of you.

Again, since the clubface tends to look in the direction in which the clubhead moves through impact, the more it swings on a straight edge instead of around a rim, the longer it will face in one direction—will hold its facing instead of turning from right to left. You'll sense this resistance to turning if you simulate the straight-edge swing with your left hand representing the clubhead, as shown in the drawing here. Be sure to start by aligning yourself to the left. Then swing your hand outside your flight path at the start of your backswing and along it on your forward swing.

FLIGHT PATH

It is this feeling of resistance to closing that you should feel in your left arm and hand when you actually swing a club. You'll probably feel that the clubface isn't closing and turning to the left as much or as quickly as it did in your old swing, unless you happened to be a chronic slicer of the ball. It's this feeling of resistance that tells you that you are keeping your clubface looking where you want it to look a bit longer through the impact area.

Sooner or later in your swing you are going to have to let the "door" close. If you didn't, you'd probably dislocate your left shoulder. I wouldn't want you to carry out the straight-edge swing to that extreme. So, remember, all we're trying to do is keep the clubface moving down the flight path *an inch or so longer* and to keep the clubface looking in the right direction just *a split second longer* than it does in the rim swing. If nothing else, I hope that by now you at least see the potential of my swing for enabling you to do both.

So far in this chapter, all I've really told you is that, under normal conditions, you should try to curve your long shots, and that the swing that keeps the clubhead moving down the flight path longer is also the swing that is more likely to keep your clubface looking in the right direction longer. The "right" direction, of course, is the direction that will give you the curve you want a particular shot to take.

Shortly, I'll tell you how to control the curve of your shots, but first I want to explain one reason why many golfers so seldom get the direction of curve, or the amount of curve, they desire. It's because they rely too heavily on their hands and wrists to generate distance on their shots.

Now, understand that there always has to be *some* wrist action in the golf swing. Whenever you're swinging something as long as a golf club at the speed a golf club moves, it is impossible to avoid some bending and unbending in the wrists, because they're forced to react to the momentum and weight of the club. The only way to avoid some sort of give in your wrists is to grip the club like a vise and swing with your arms stiff, and anyone who tries that won't hit the ball past first base.

The biggest problem in golf for most players, however, is that they get *too much* wrist action in the *wrong* way at the *wrong* time. That's one big reason why golfers mis-hit so many shots. Since your hands can directly influence your clubhead, the more wrist action you have, the greater the chance that your hands are going to either throw it out of its proper path or flip or roll the clubface into the wrong alignment at impact. It's as simple as that.

Too much wrist action can flip the clubface closed to the left, or open to the right, as it moves into the impact area. Too much wrist action can throw the clubhead into the ground behind the ball or, more often, flip it up into the air so that you top the shot. Too much wrist action often throws the clubhead onto an outside rim during the downswing, so that it cuts across the flight path instead of moving directly down it through the ball. Too much wrist action too soon in your downswing can cause you to waste clubhead speed before impact. And too much wrist action can cause you to loosen your hold on the club at the top of your backswing.

It's also the hands and wrists that so often let you down under pressure. They are quick reactors, and too often they react in the wrong way or at the wrong time. Anytime you start swinging at that golf ball with those hands and wrists on a pressure shot, I'll guarantee you can miss the world with it.

I remember one time when I was leading the Houston Open, back in 1968 before I'd won my first U.S. Open. I was coming down the stretch, gasping like an old hound dog in heat, and, naturally I'd just bogeyed the seventeenth hole. I had a 3-iron shot to the last hole and I didn't have any idea where it was going to go because I just slapped at it with my hands. I left all the pressure to my hands, and I couldn't have hit that green if it had been as big as the Astrodome. I didn't win that tournament, and I lost several others before I learned how to keep my wrist action quiet under pressure.

As I say, most people have more than enough wrist action already. I suppose extra wrist action can give you a few yards more distance, but only if you time it perfectly. I know that I, for one, don't have that much talent. And I play golf for a living. If you only play once or twice a week, you have *no chance* trying to flick shots with your hands. In the old days when golfers tied their arms up in dress shirts and heavy jackets, they may have needed more wrist action to get adequate distance, but it's certainly not the way to play consistent, accurate golf today in double-knit slacks and light shirts. For every shot you hit a bit farther with extra wrist action, you'll lose distance on a dozen others because you won't make solid contact with the ball.

So, many golfers need to tame, or train, their wrist action in order to make their clubface look in the right direction through impact. I've found that there are two things you can do to keep your hands and wrists quiet, but not stiff or wooden, as you swing. These two things more or less tie in together, in that if you do one of them it makes it easier to do the other. And both these remedies for excessive wristiness are valid because you can still swing naturally as you apply them. In other words, you don't need to slow anything down, or resort to some unnatural steering or guiding of the clubhead, to make them work.

The two things I'm talking about are left-hand control and forward acceleration. Let's take left-hand control first.

LEFT-HAND CONTROL

To understand what left-hand control is all about, take a pencil in your left hand (right hand for southpaws) and hold it in front of you as you would a golf club. At first, hold the pencil as lightly as you can. Then flip your hand at the wrist. Flip it back and forth, up and down, around in a circle, any way you can. You can see how easy it is to maneuver the pencil with just your hand and wrist, without hardly moving your arm.

The reason it's so easy to move the pencil all over the place is that you're holding it so lightly. With this light hold, you have very little left-hand control. Imagine swinging a golf club at top speed with this same amount of grip pressure, and you can sense how easy it would be for your hands and wrists to let the clubface turn off line, flip upward, bury in the ground, or whatever. In short, you can see immediately how too little left-hand control can make your golf swing too wristy, and thereby very difficult for you to keep the clubface looking in the right direction during impact.

Let's now try another experiment. Squeeze that same pencil as hard as you possibly can with the last three fingers of your left hand. Really give it a Charles Atlas grip. Now try moving the pencil. See how difficult it is to move with just your hand and wrist? See how much easier it is to move the pencil by using your whole left arm instead? And, as you move your arm back and forth, you can see how much easier it is to *control* the pencil, to avoid flipping it up and down or back and forth or around in a circle with your wrist.

This is left-hand control in the extreme. You wouldn't want to hold the club this tightly as you actually addressed and swung at a golf ball, because that much pressure would restrict your action terribly. But the pressure you now feel in your left-hand fingers should give you an idea of how left-hand control can help minimize excessive manipulation of the clubface, and help you to keep it looking where you want it to look through impact.

I suspect that many of my fellow pros will disagree with all this. I've heard many of them assert that "golf is a two-handed game." Some have even said or written that they get their power from the right hand. Well, I'm sure they are sincere, but I don't think they realize the tremendous *left-hand* control they've built up over the years of hitting several hundred thousand golf shots.

I agree that the right hand is necessary to some extent in golf

61

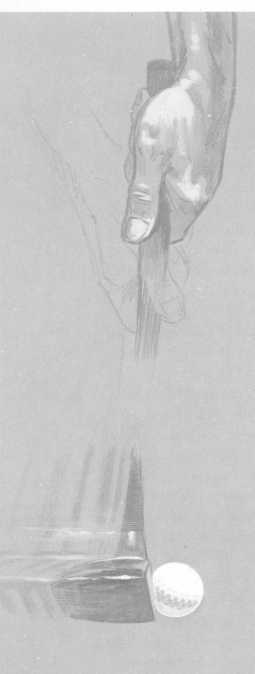

LEFT-HAND DOMINANCE

While golf is a two-handed game, most golfers need more control of the club with the left hand. Holding on firmly with the last three fingers of this hand helps to keep the clubface looking in the proper direction through impact.

RIGHT-HAND DOMINANCE

Too much right-hand dominance, or too little left-hand control, allows the right hand to take over during the downswing. Then, during impact, it will have misaligned the clubface, and also perhaps have flipped the clubhead upward into the ball.

(I'd sure hate to play with only my left hand on the club), but I also feel that for most weekend golfers too much right-hand dominance—or, better yet, too little left-hand control—is the major reason why they find it so difficult to put that clubface solidly into the back of the ball with any sort of consistency.

Golf *is* a two-handed game, but it's a lot easier to be a consistent golfer if only one hand is in *control*. I vote for the left hand because, the more your right hand dominates your left as you swing, the more you're probably going to flip the clubhead out of proper position with your wrists. It's as simple as that.

FORWARD ACCELERATION

The second element you need to keep from becoming too wristy is forward acceleration. Take a club in your hands and try flicking the clubhead through the impact area primarily with your wrists. I'll bet what happens is that, as the clubhead swings forward and upward, your arms almost come to a stop, and that your left wrist breaks down—cups inward—just above the back of your hand.

What's happened here is that you've put yourself into a very weak impact position, because your clubhead has outraced your hands back to the ball. This is wrong—your hands should *always* win this race. At impact your left hand should always be slightly ahead of your clubface with, if anything, the back of your left wrist bowed outward slightly, not cupped inward. I'll get into why this is ideal in more detail later when I talk about keeping the clubhead at ball level and getting maximum distance on your shots. But, for now, just let me say that, in terms of keeping your clubface looking in the right direction, the bowed-left-wrist impact position is one heck of a lot better than the cupped-wrist position.

The reason your arms slowed down and your left wrist cupped

63

ACCELERATION AIDS
LEFT-HAND CONTROL

Left-hand control through impact is more likely to occur if the left arm continues accelerating forward. Such acceleration is more likely to happen if you slide laterally at the start of your downswing and thereby drop the club onto an inside rim. Starting

ALIGNING LEFT =

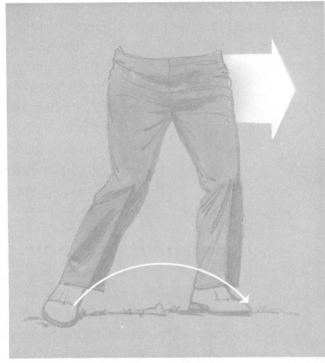

LATERAL SLIDE =

ALIGNING RIGHT =

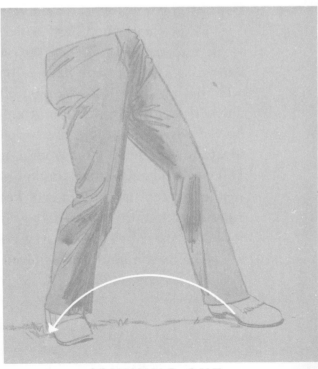

SPINNING OUT =

out by aligning to the left makes the lateral slide much easier. This chain reaction is shown in the top row of drawings. The bottom row shows the opposite set of reactions: aligning to the right forces you to spin to the left—back toward your target—which causes spinning instead of lateral sliding; the spinning produces a left-arm deceleration, which gives the right hand a chance to take over and misalign the clubface and/or flip it upward.

LEFT-ARM ACCELERATION   =   LEFT-HAND CONTROL

LEFT-ARM DECELERATION   =   RIGHT-HAND CONTROL

was that you tried to flick the shot with your wrists. Hitting with the hands and wrists causes everything else—arms, hips, legs—to *decelerate.*

On the other hand, if you can learn to *accelerate* your left arm, hips, and legs as you swing into the ball, you leave yourself very little chance to overuse your hands and wrists. It all ties together: the more you lead your downswing turn with your hips and legs sliding laterally, the easier it becomes to make your left arm continue to accelerate into the impact area. The more your left arm accelerates forward, the easier it is for your left hand to beat the clubface back to the ball. And making your left hand win that race is the best way to retain left-hand control of the club, and to avoid flipping the clubface out of proper alignment with the wrists.

Let's say it again just to make sure you understand. Too much wrist action misaligns your clubface and flips the clubhead to the outside rim. Too much wrist action comes from too little left-hand control—or too much right-hand effort. Extra grip pressure in the last two or three fingers of your left hand creates more left-hand control. Accelerating the arms, as a result of making your legs and hips slide laterally, helps you retain this control.

The point I want to make now is that left-hand control and forward acceleration really result from the first thing I told you that I do when getting ready to hit a golf shot. *By aligning myself 30 to 40 degrees to the left of my initial flight path as I address the ball, I set myself in position to accelerate.*

The more you align yourself to the *right* at address, the farther your hips and shoulders are going to be aligned to the right of target at the top of your backswing. Also, the more you're aligned to the right, the farther you're going to swing the clubhead off your flight path, to the inside, during your backswing. You're also likely to roll the clubface open to the right as you swing the clubhead back to the inside. Thus, at the top of the backswing, you've got yourself aligned way to the right of target, your clubhead is far inside the flight path, and your clubface is probably open, in perfect position for hitting a big slice.

What do you do from there? You want to slide your hips and legs laterally to the left so that you can build up some arm acceleration and maintain left-hand control. But you can't make this slide because, if you did, your left hip and leg would be in the way and block your arms from swinging down the flight path. You'd get arm acceleration if you made the slide, but your arms would be accelerating out to the right of where you want the ball to go.

So aligning to the right at address makes it difficult to slide laterally to the left in your downswing, as you need to do to get left-arm acceleration to maintain left-hand control. If you do slide, you also must put a tremendous amount of hand and wrist action into your downswing to make the clubface return to proper alignment by impact. And, as I've said, the hands and wrists alone don't do that job very well very often.

However, if you align to the left at address as I do, you *can* slide laterally with your hips and legs as you start your downswing turn without leaving your left side in the way of your arms. The arms then *can* accelerate forward so that you'll be able to retain left-hand control and avoid the excessive wristiness that can misalign the clubface.

If you need any further convincing that aligning to the left makes it easier to accelerate forward through impact, and thus reduce wristiness, let me tell you about something I do to help golfers with their putting.

I find that many people putt badly because they don't keep their left hand and arm accelerating out toward the hole, or, on a breaking putt, down the initial path where they want the ball to roll. They decelerate, and as a result the putterhead flips upward or off line.

What I do is set a ball down on the green about twenty feet away from the pupil. Then I ask the pupil to set up to putt another ball toward it. I tell him to hold that setup position, and then I move the target ball about ten feet to the right. What I've now done, in effect, is to get the pupil and his putterface aligned and aimed way to the left of his target, but then I make him putt toward the target ball from that position.

What happens when he does this is that he makes the best putting stroke you'd ever want to see, because he's now *forced* to accelerate his left arm and hand through the ball and out toward his target. With this acceleration, his left wrist can't cup inward. That keeps his putterhead square and moving out and down the line low to the ground. It doesn't turn left, swing left, or flip upward.

For maybe the first time in his life the golfer gets a feeling of a good putting stroke, all because I forced him into an open alignment and made him aim to the left. I don't recommend you do this on all of your putts, because that would be too confusing, but I *would* suggest you try this drill if you're having trouble making yourself accelerate forward during your stroke—at least until you get the *feeling* of acceleration and of the left-hand control that results from it.

HOW TO GRIP

By now you may have wondered how to grip the club and where to aim it. These questions need to be answered, because the way you position your hands on the club and where you aim the clubface heavily influence where your clubface is going to be looking when you hit the ball.

I think the best way you can hold the club is by simply making sure that the back of your left hand is parallel with the leading edge of the clubface. Once you get the back of the hand and the leading edge set up in the same direction, you don't need to worry about where your clubface is going to be looking during impact. Instead, all you need to think about is where the *back of your left hand* is going to be facing as you strike the ball.

I think it's a lot easier for most golfers to control the facing of their left hand than the clubface itself. Just marry the two at address, then swing the back of your left hand wherever you want your clubface to be looking at impact.

The best way to get the left hand aligned with the clubface is to stand with your hands at your sides, with your palms facing inward. Have someone position the club in front of you so that the shaft comes up from behind the ball toward the seam of the slacks on your left thigh. Next simply bring your left hand forward to grip the club. Set your left thumb just slightly to the top-right side of the shaft and close your fingers around it, making sure that the back of your hand aligns with the leading edge of the clubface. When you close your fingers, you should find that the "V" that formed between your thumb and forefinger points up to somewhere between your right cheek and your right shoulder. This gives you the ideal left-hand grip position.

If you'll now lift the club slightly off the ground with only the last three fingers of this hand, you'll immediately feel the proper firmness needed in these fingers to maintain maximum left-hand control throughout the swing.

Next, bring your right hand forward as if you were going to complete your grip. Before you close this hand around the club, however, lay the "lifeline" of that palm straight down the top of your left thumb. Next, position your right thumb to run down the top of your clubshaft in such a way that the end of the thumb rests just slightly on the top-left side of the club. You should find that the "V" of your right hand also points upward toward the space between your right cheek and right shoulder—in other words, in about the same direction as the left-hand "V," or maybe a little bit more toward your right shoulder.

FOUR STEPS TO A PROPER GRIP

The grip that I suggest you use is one in which the back of your top hand—left hand for righthanders—faces in the same direction as does the leading edge of the clubface. Then, as you swing through the ball, you can automatically control the direction the clubhead faces with the back of this leading hand.

STEP 1 *Stand upright with your hands at your sides and your palms facing your legs.*

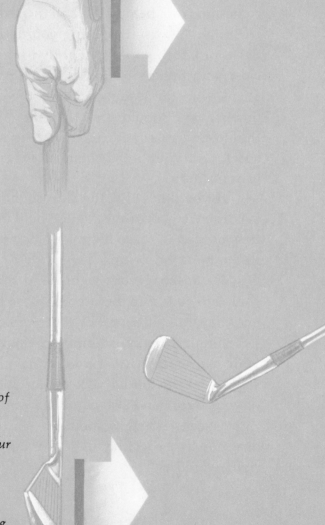

STEP 2 *Have someone position the club in front of you with its leading edge set just inside your left heel and facing down your flight path so that the shaft runs up toward the seam of the slacks on your left thigh. Bring your left hand forward and set it on the club so that your thumb rests on the top right side of the shaft, and the back of your left hand aligns with the leading edge of the clubface. Close your fingers around the club without altering this alignment as you do so.*

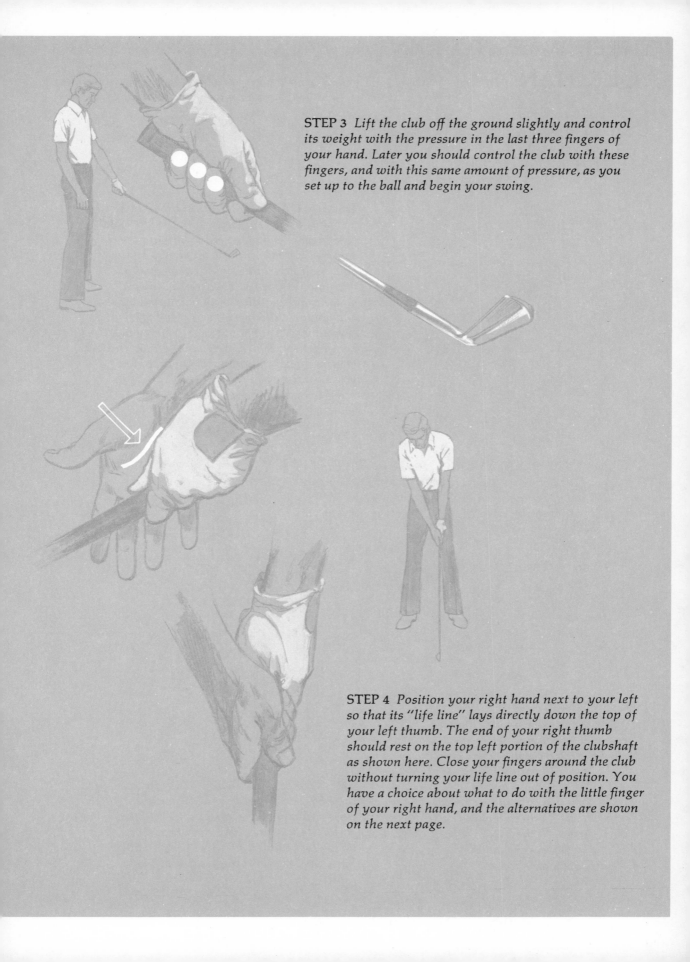

STEP 3 *Lift the club off the ground slightly and control its weight with the pressure in the last three fingers of your hand. Later you should control the club with these fingers, and with this same amount of pressure, as you set up to the ball and begin your swing.*

STEP 4 *Position your right hand next to your left so that its "life line" lays directly down the top of your left thumb. The end of your right thumb should rest on the top left portion of the clubshaft as shown here. Close your fingers around the club without turning your life line out of position. You have a choice about what to do with the little finger of your right hand, and the alternatives are shown on the next page.*

THREE WAYS TO JOIN YOUR HANDS

On the preceding pages I showed you the basic steps in proper gripping. Here we see three ways to finally meld your hands together. The choice is up to you, but let me explain a few things about each.

THE 10-FINGER GRIP   *Here the right hand's little finger does not meld with the left hand's forefinger. They merely wrap around the club side by side, thus putting all fingers on the club itself. I feel this type of grip gives maximum control of the club and thus is good for people with weak hands and wrists, and golfers with overly-wristy swings. I sometimes use it out of rough, where I want firmer wrists. By reducing wrist action, this grip might cost you some distance, but not if you need the extra club control it offers in order to make more solid contact.*

THE OVERLAP GRIP   *Here the right hand's little finger laps over the left hand's forefinger. This grip is used by 99 percent of good golfers. It provides slightly more control in the left hand.*

THE INTERLOCK GRIP   *This grip finds the little finger of the right hand interlocking with the forefinger of the left. It's the grip that Jack Nicklaus uses, so it can't be too bad. Actually, I think it's fine for people with small hands and/or short fingers (as Jack has).*

When you close the fingers of your right hand, all but your little finger will wrap around the clubshaft. What you do with your little finger depends on what type of grip you want to make—overlap, interlock, or ten-finger.

With the overlap type of grip, the little finger of your right hand laps over the forefinger of your left hand. This takes the little finger of the right hand off the clubshaft, which slightly weakens the right hand's hold on the club, and also unifies the hands. For those reasons it is used by 99 percent of golfers, including me.

If you want to try the interlock grip, instead of lapping the little finger of your right hand over the forefinger of your left, simply intertwine the two so that both fingers are off the club. Jack Nicklaus is one of the few golfers who interlock. I prefer the more popular overlap grip, but when the best player in the world interlocks, who can say it's wrong? Actually, the interlocking grip works fine for golfers with small hands, which Jack has. I don't think it works so well if you have long fingers.

In the ten-finger grip, the little finger of the right hand simply wraps around the club along with all of the other fingers, neither overlapping nor interlocking with the forefinger of the left hand. I think the ten-finger grip is good for someone who doesn't have very much grip strength, because it does tend to make you less wristy as you swing. I use it on shots out of deep rough where I want my wrists firmer and my hold on the club tighter than normal. I think this grip is also good for weak-wristed women and children who have trouble controlling the club while swinging. The drawback, however, is that it can reduce distance because it cuts down on wrist action.

I wouldn't quarrel with any of these grips so long as they keep your hands together as a unit, but I do think the overlap gives most people their best chance for maximum left-hand control.

The most important grip factor as I see it is that you align the back of your left hand with the leading edge of the clubface, so that the club will always face wherever you make the back of your hand face. I think this hand-clubface alignment also gives you your best chance for making your hands return to a strong position at impact. By a "strong" position, I again mean one in which the left hand leads the clubface slightly in the race back to the ball.

Now, I know that some readers are going to say that Trevino doesn't practice what he preaches when it comes to aligning the left hand and the clubface. In a sense they'd be right because, while I do start out by holding the club with the back of my left hand aligned with the leading edge of the face, I then regrip just before I start the clubhead back—I turn my hands slightly to my right on the club without changing the aiming of the clubface.

I do this for two reasons. First, it's a way I have of breaking tension in my hands and arms. Second, it puts my hands in a position that would cause me to hook the ball badly to the left if I should happen to roll my wrists too much to the left through impact. Here again, by regripping into a hooker's grip, I put myself on the "brink of disaster" so that I'll be sure to react in only one way—in a way that keeps me from "closing the door" with my clubface through impact. In short, the hooker's grip forces me not to let the clubface close, and that again helps to keep it looking in the same direction as it is traveling a little bit longer through impact.

But this regripping is an idiosyncrasy that I wouldn't expect, or want, anyone else to try. Regripping would probably ruin another golfer's sense of rhythm or his sense of clubface control. I mention it here only to explain why my grip doesn't quite look the way I'm telling you yours should look.

The last thing I want to emphasize about gripping, which I do stress in my own game, is that, as you hold the club, you should feel that you're controlling it primarily in the last three fingers of your left hand. Keep your right hand very soft on the club. And, if you waggle the clubhead before you swing, make sure you do the waggling chiefly with these last three fingers of your left hand.

74

Lee Trevino

What you never want to happen during the swing is any grabbing of the club with the right hand. If your right hand takes over on the backswing, it's got to tighten that arm and block you from dropping the club into the slot—onto the inside rim—as you slide laterally during your downswing turn. Or, if you grab with your right hand at the start of the downswing, you'll probably throw or shove the clubhead onto the outside rim.

So be sure you control the clubshaft with the last three fingers of your left hand, both at address and throughout your swing. Hold that right hand on there as though you're drinking champagne out of Tiffany stemware. The only time you might want to increase your right-hand grip pressure at address is when you're hooking the ball badly, when extra pressure at address will often keep you from grabbing on tighter and throwing the clubface closed during your downswing.

WHERE TO AIM

Some readers might feel that aligning the back of the left hand with the leading edge of the clubface, as I suggest, will make slicers out of many golfers. They might feel that this "aligned" grip isn't "strong" enough for them to get the clubface back to "square" by impact. I suppose this would be true except for one factor: *in my system, you determine the way your shot is going to curve in flight by where you aim the clubface and align yourself at address.*

When it comes to aiming the clubface, I'm going to give you a real shocker. I'm sure you've all heard or read that you should aim the clubface down your initial flight path, or directly at your target, if you're trying to make a straight shot.

Well, aiming the clubface down the flight path is standard instruction only because everyone is teaching a square stance and body alignment at address. Aiming down the flight path does make sense if you're setting up square and trying to make the old "rim swing," back and forward around the edge of the half-football I described.

However, aiming the clubface more or less down the flight path won't work if you're going to try my system. I've got myself aligned 30 to 40 degrees left of my initial flight path at address. But then I'm going to swing my clubhead down and out *along* that initial flight path through impact. If I aimed the face, and my left hand, down that path originally, by the time the clubface got back to the ball it would have to be looking 30 to 40 degrees to the *right* of my flight path.

What I'm saying is that, if you're going to align yourself 30 to 40 degrees to the left of your flight path at address, *you've also got to aim your clubface, and the back of your left hand, to the left.*

I know that aiming the clubface to the left of where you want your ball to go is going to sound crazy to the "rim swingers," but I think it makes sense. It makes sense because what we're trying to do at impact is keep the clubface looking down the line a bit longer than normal.

We particularly don't want it to roll closed to the left too soon in the impact area. Now, the more you aim to the *right*, as many golfers do subconsciously, the more you're going to roll or flip that clubface closed to the left through impact. The more you aim to the *left*, however, the less you're likely to roll the clubface left through impact. Instead of closing the door, you'll try to keep it open a bit longer.

Why? I think it all has to do with human reaction. We react instinctively to the facing of the club. If we sense that the clubface is going to be looking to the right at impact, we'll react by rolling our hands to the left. This keeps the clubface from looking forward for a very long span—if at all—through impact. But if we feel that the clubface is *already* looking to the left, we'll instinctively do everything we can to avoid rolling it even farther to the left. And, in my

YOU REACT IN YOUR SWING
TO WHERE YOU'VE AIMED

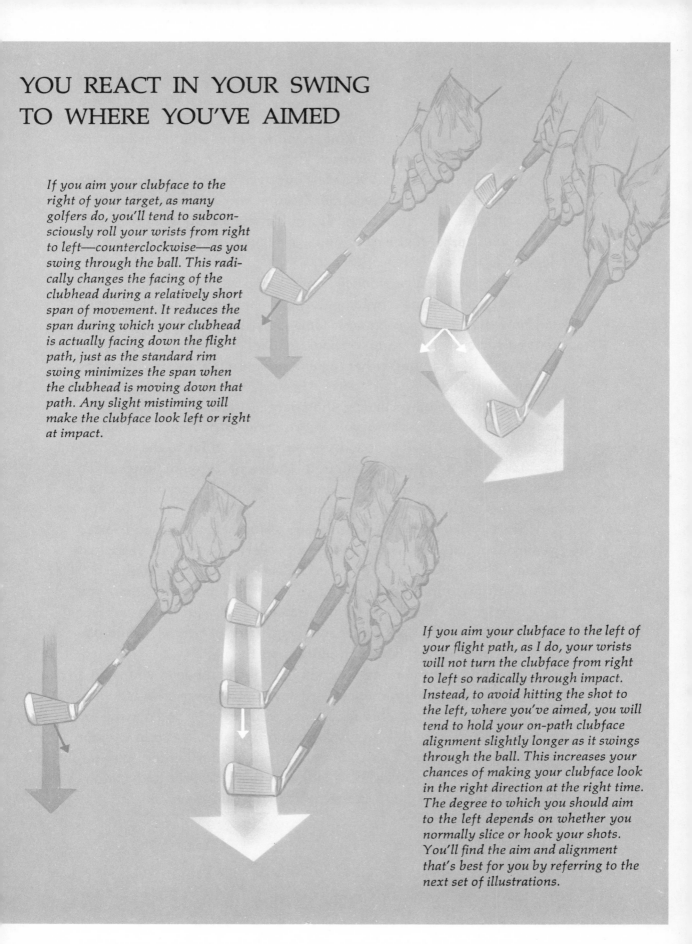

If you aim your clubface to the right of your target, as many golfers do, you'll tend to subconsciously roll your wrists from right to left—counterclockwise—as you swing through the ball. This radically changes the facing of the clubhead during a relatively short span of movement. It reduces the span during which your clubhead is actually facing down the flight path, just as the standard rim swing minimizes the span when the clubhead is moving down that path. Any slight mistiming will make the clubface look left or right at impact.

If you aim your clubface to the left of your flight path, as I do, your wrists will not turn the clubface from right to left so radically through impact. Instead, to avoid hitting the shot to the left, where you've aimed, you will tend to hold your on-path clubface alignment slightly longer as it swings through the ball. This increases your chances of making your clubface look in the right direction at the right time. The degree to which you should aim to the left depends on whether you normally slice or hook your shots. You'll find the aim and alignment that's best for you by referring to the next set of illustrations.

case, that's what keeps it looking down the line, where I want it to look, a bit longer through impact.

What I suggest is that you start out by aiming your club and the back of your left hand in the same direction you've aligned your feet, hips, and shoulders at address. If you've aligned 30 degrees to the left of your initial flight path, aim your hand and club the same 30 degrees to the left.

Then, after you've practiced my swing pattern for a while, using the grip I suggest, the aim I suggest, and the swing I suggest, check out how the ball curves on your long shots. If your shots are slicing too much from left to right, or hooking badly from right to left, you can correct by changing either the aim of your clubface or your body alignment at address.

Let's say you are curving shots largely from left to right. You may be doing this because you are reacting to having the clubface looking so far to the left at address—aiming it so far to the left may be making you actually open it to the right through impact. To eliminate this reaction, merely address the ball with your clubface aimed *less* to the left.

If this change of aim doesn't cure your slicing, then go back to aiming the club the same degree to the left as you had been, but change the alignment of your feet and body. Make them align *less* to the left at address. By aligning yourself less to the left than you are aiming, you'll tend to swing into the ball with your clubface looking to the left of where it's swinging. This, of course, would off-set any slice spin you had been putting on the ball.

If you've been curving your shots badly to the left, you should try just the opposite procedure. First try aiming your clubface *more* to the left at address. This may make you react in your swing by reducing your wrist roll in that direction. You'll fear rolling your clubface to the left because you've already aimed farther left. Instead, you'll hold the door open a bit longer through impact and thereby eliminate the closed clubface that was giving you the hook.

If aiming farther left doesn't help your hooking, go back to your original aim but align your feet and body *more* to the left. This, in effect, sets your clubface to the right of where you're aligned, which helps to prevent it from looking to the left of its path—in the hooking position—during impact.

The reason I've given you two different ways to correct for slicing and two for hooking is that I can't be sure just how you, as an individual, will react to aiming the clubface to the left at address. It might take some experimentation to find out which of the two alternatives works best for you.

What I do suggest, however, is that you first try to find the combination of clubface aim and body alignment at address that gives you a *slight* amount of curve, and in the same direction, on most of your long shots. Work to develop a consistent "shape" of shot, either left to right or right to left. Don't worry if the curve is bigger on some shots than on others; that's going to happen to all of us. All we're trying to do is to find the relationship of aim and alignment that gives us the same direction of curve, but not too much curve, most of the time.

When you find a consistent shape to your shots, then you can count on basically playing for that shape on the course, even under pressure. And I promise you that this will lead immediately to lower scores.

For most readers, learning to shape shots in one direction only will be about as far as they'll want to go. Better players, however, may want to learn to shape shots in either direction, a left-to-right fade or a right-to-left draw, so that they can play the best shape for any particular shot at hand.

The beauty of my system is that you can determine the shape of your shot before you swing, merely by adjusting where you aim the clubface in relation to where you align yourself. Then you can go ahead and make the same swing every time. I think this is bound to make most golfers more consistent.

FINDING THE AIM
THAT'S BEST FOR YOU

30°   30°

You have two choices when it comes to altering the way your shots curve in the air. You can either change your alignment, by aligning your feet and body more or less to the left than you have been; or you can change the direction in which you're aiming the back of your left hand and, thus, your clubface alignment. Since every player swings a bit differently from everyone else, I can't tell you exactly where to align and aim, so I'll give you some general guidelines on these pages. I do suggest, however, that you start by aligning your feet and body about the same amount to the left of your flight path as you aim the back of your left hand and the clubface. You'll notice this relationship is shown in the drawing above, where everything is aligned and aimed 30 degrees left of the flight path.

TO DECREASE HOOKING, AIM FARTHER LEFT   *It may sound strange to aim farther left to cure shots that are already flying too far to the left. However, as I explained earlier, if you aim farther left, you will instinctively prevent your wrists from rolling the clubface to the left, which is what causes hooking in the first place.*

TO DECREASE SLICING, ALIGN LESS TO THE LEFT   *You may be slicing from left to right because your clubhead is swinging down to the ball along an outside rim, thereby cutting across the ball and giving it a left-to-right side-spin. By aligning your feet and body less to the left, you'll improve your chances of swinging back to the ball from inside to along your flight path.*

TO DECREASE SLICING, AIM LESS TO THE LEFT   *The less you aim the clubface to the left, the less you'll fear hitting the ball to the left. This will cause you to react by rolling your wrists more freely from right to left through the impact area. The extra wrist-rolling will help cure slicing.*

TO DECREASE HOOKING, ALIGN MORE TO THE LEFT   *If your hooking comes from swinging back to the ball on a rim that's too far inside your flight path, aligning farther to the left will bring that path back to normal. The normal clubhead path will reduce your wrist-rolling to the left, which had been causing your hooking in that direction.*

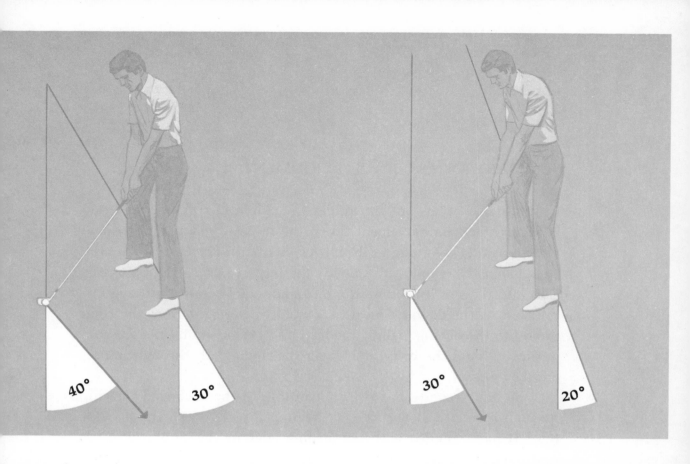

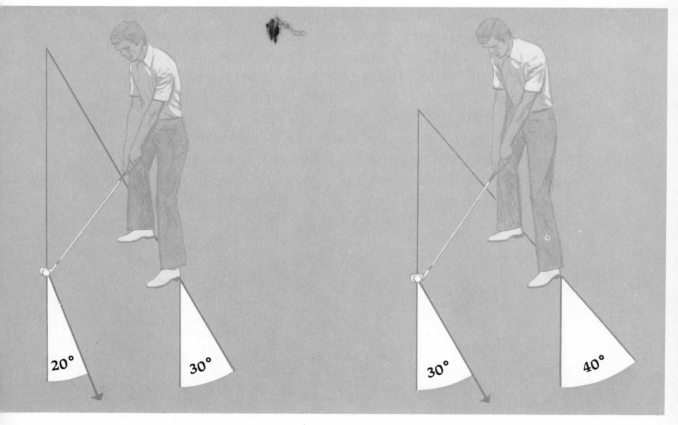

SUMMARY OF CLUBFACE ALIGNMENT

In the first chapter, on controlling the clubhead's path, I told you how to extend its movement down the initial flight path by doing four things: (1) aligning to the left of that path; (2) starting the club back along this alignment, outside the flight path; (3) dropping the club into the slot by sliding the hips and legs laterally to the left at the start of the downswing turn, by shifting weight from the right foot onto the outside ball of the left; and (4) extending the left arm out away from the body and down the flight path through impact and beyond.

In this second chapter, on controlling the clubhead's facing through impact, I suggested: (1) holding the club with the back of the left hand aligned with the leading edge of the clubface; (2) at first aiming the clubface in the same direction you've aligned, and then modifying this relationship according to the curve you want your shots to take; (3) controlling the club with the last three fingers of your left hand, both at address and throughout the swing, and (4) maintaining this left-hand control by *accelerating* your hips, legs, and left arm forward as you swing through impact.

Remember, it's left-hand control combined with swinging the clubhead on line longer that keeps the clubface looking in the right direction longer through impact. It's left-arm acceleration that helps you maintain left-hand control. And it's the open alignment and the lateral slide that allow you to make this acceleration.

3 FINDING BALL LEVEL

THIS CHAPTER IS ABOUT the third of the major elements of my swing that help me come close to my target on most of my shots. This third element is what keeps me from topping one shot and then burying the clubhead behind the ball on the next. It is the element of making the clubhead swing through the impact area while it's traveling more or less at *ball level*.

This is important, because it is possible to swing your clubhead down the flight path (Chapter 1), and make your clubface look in the right direction (Chapter 2), and *still* outdrive your ball with your divot, or even fan the ball completely. You can swing down the flight path all day, with your clubhead as square as Lawrence Welk, but you're not going to win many Nassaus if you're skulling one shot and drop-kicking the next.

Unless you happen to be playing off your knees your clubhead *must* swing upward on your backswing, downward on your downswing, and then back up again on your follow-through. Thus it's going to be near ball level for only an instant between your downswing and your follow-through. However, the more you can extend that span of ball-level clubhead movement, the better your chances are for making solid contact. Also, the longer you make that span the bigger margin you'll have against any error you might have made in positioning the ball too far forward or too far back in your stance.

First, I'm going to tell you why doing the things I've already suggested you do is likely, in itself, to increase this span of ball-level clubhead movement. Then I'll help you find the proper ball position for your particular swing.

Except possibly on drives, where the ball sets up on a peg, your clubhead should either be descending very slightly or sweeping level to the ground through impact. If it's already starting to move upward, you run the risk of topping, or at least "thinning," shots. The slightly descending approach to the ball helps protect you against that problem.

On the other hand, you don't want the clubhead chopping too sharply downward to the ball. Too much descent can either stick the clubhead into the ground behind the ball or smash down on top of it. Also, with such a steep downward blow, too much of your force goes into the ground instead of forward, where you want the shot to go. Thus, you lose some distance, even when you make fairly solid contact.

The factor that has a lot to do with your clubhead's angle of attack is the "rim" it happens to be moving along in your downswing. You'll see what I mean if you can imagine: (1) a clockface and (2) a half-circle of the same diameter. Visualize the half-circle setting perfectly upright, on the center of its curved rim on the center of the clockface, so that its straight edge extends from the 6 to the 12 of the face (see illustration). Also imagine that a golf ball is in the center of the face, where the curved rim is touching. Imagine that you're going to play a shot to "12 o'clock." Assuming you're right-handed, that means that you'd be standing on the left side of the half-circle, between the center of the clockface and the number 9.

84

Now, imagine that the rim of the half-circle indicates the angle of downward and upward movement your clubhead is going to make before and after impact. When you look at this rim, you'll notice two things. First, because the half-circle is setting perfectly upright, the clubhead is always moving down the flight path, in this case from 6 to 12 on the clockface. At the same time, however, it's moving either downward or upward most of the way. It's at ball level for only a very short span between downswing and follow-through.

What this means is that, if you could swing on a perfectly upright or vertical plane, like that formed by the perfectly upright half-circle, your chances of starting your shots out in the right direction would be excellent, because your clubhead would always be moving down your flight path. However, with such an upright swing plane, your clubhead would not be at ball level very long, thus your chances of making solid contact would be pretty slim.

Now, visualize keeping your half-circle setting on the middle of its rim in the center of the clockface, but gradually tilt its top edge to your left—toward the number 9 on the clockface. Keep tilting it down until the half-circle is lying flat on the clockface with the center of its rim still touching the center of the clock (see illustration).

When the half-circle is lying flat like this, it represents a perfectly *flat* swing plane. This is the type of plane you'd get if your clubhead never left ground level during your swing.

Obviously, this would be a great swing—if you could physically perform it—for keeping the clubhead at ball level and for making solid contact in that respect. But look at that rim and see how short a span that the clubhead would be actually moving *down the flight path*. Instead of swinging from the 6 to the 12 on the clock, now it would only momentarily touch the flight path as it moved from somewhere between 7 and 8 to somewhere between 10 and 11.

The first point I'm making here is simply that the more *upright* the plane of your forward swing, the *more* the clubhead moves down the flight path, but the *less* it stays at ball level. Conversely,

"PLANE" FACTS ABOUT SOLID CONTACT

The plane on which your golf club swings has much to do with whether or not it comes into impact with the clubhead moving at ball level and along the flight path. If you imagine a half-football setting vertically on a clockface and extending from "6 o'clock" to "12 o'clock" (drawings at rignt), you can see how a perfectly vertical plane would keep the clubhead on the flight path throughout, but at ball level all too briefly to assure solid contact. Swinging down to the ball on an outside rim can make your plane so vertical that the force of the blow is downward into the ground instead of forward toward your target. The result is a great loss of distance.

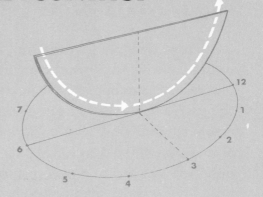

A perfectly flat swing plane, as shown in the drawings on the right, would keep the clubhead moving at ball level throughout, but the clubhead would be moving down the flight path only for an instant. Chances are slim that your shots would then start out in the right direction and fly straight. The force of the blow would not be too much downward, as discussed above, but too much to the left or right of your flight path.

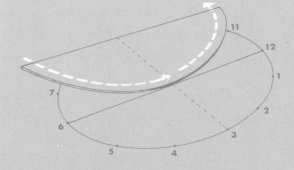

In the standard golf swing the plane on which the club swings is somewhere between the two extremes shown above. Ideally, it's flat enough to keep the clubhead moving more or less at ball level through impact, yet upright enough to make sure that it's moving down the flight path at the same time. If you will turn the page, I'll show how I make my clubhead stay at ball level longer without decreasing the span of its movement down the flight path.

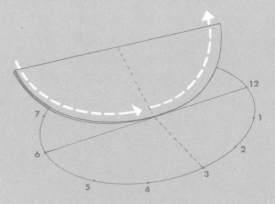

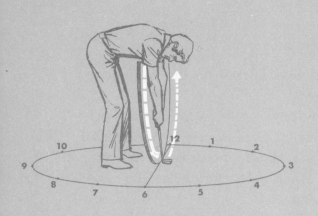

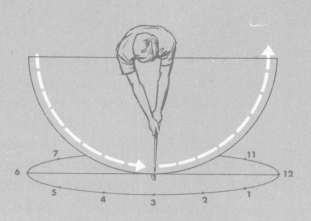

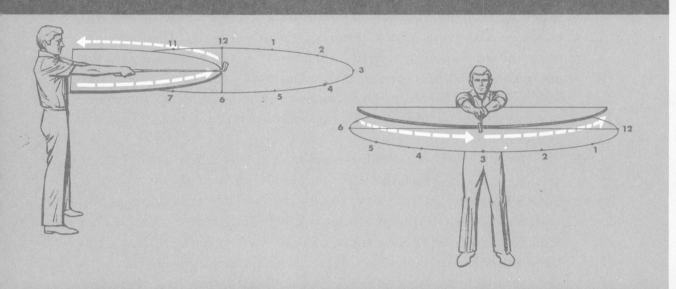

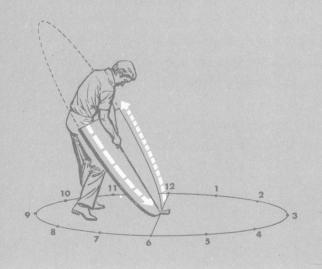

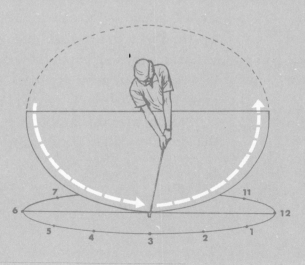

the *flatter* the plane, the *less* the clubhead stays on the flight path, but the *more* it stays at ball level.

Of course, no golfer can swing on a perfectly upright or perfectly flat plane. Everyone swings on a plane that's somewhere in between. If you tilted the half-circle about one-third of the way downward from perfectly upright, you'd get more or less the plane on which most golfers actually swing.

The second point that I want you to keep in mind is that the *flatter* you make your *downswing* plane, the *shallower* your clubhead's path *into* the ball will be. This means that, if you want your clubhead to move into the ball with only a slight angle of descent, you've got to swing it back to the ball on an *inside* rim. The more you shove or throw your clubhead onto an *outside* rim coming down, the more vertical or upright you make your plane, and the steeper your angle of attack becomes. The steeper your angle of attack, the more the force of your blow goes downward instead of forward, and the less distance you get.

Now, do you remember how to make the clubhead return on an inside rim? You'll recall that in Chapter 1 I explained how I do this by sliding my hips and legs laterally to the left at the start of my downswing turn, initiating the move by shifting weight onto the outside ball of my left foot instead of onto my left heel. In short, you need this lateral slide to drop your clubhead onto an inside rim, so it will approach the ball at the correct angle of attack. But there is a slight drawback here.

The problem concerns what I've just shown you with the half-circles, which is that the more you swing down on an inside rim to get the fairly shallow, almost level angle of approach to the ball that you want, the less your clubhead can move toward it from along your flight path, but must approach the ball more from inside that path—more from "7 o'clock" instead of "6 o'clock."

I minimize this problem in my swing by aligning myself more to the left of my flight path at address than almost any other golfer. The

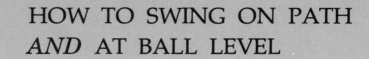

HOW TO SWING ON PATH *AND* AT BALL LEVEL

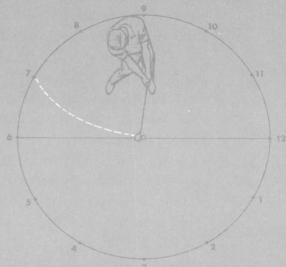

Both the golfer shown above and myself, shown below, are hitting shots toward "12 o'clock." However, you'll see that my clubhead comes into the ball on a slightly shallower angle of approach. Also, my clubhead has moved along the flight path slightly longer prior to impact. Therefore, I'm more likely to catch the ball solidly, with my clubhead moving in the right direction and at ball level. The one reason I enjoy these benefits is simply because I aligned myself and aimed my clubface toward "11 o'clock" instead of "12 o'clock" as I addressed the ball.

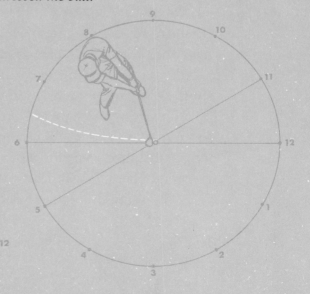

more I align, say, toward the 11 on the clockface, instead of the 12, the more I can swing my clubhead into the ball from the 6 instead of the 7, even though my downswing plane is just as flat—my angle of approach just as shallow—as the next fellow's.

Thus by aligning to the left at address, and by sliding laterally at the start of my downswing, I achieve the best of two worlds. I get the fairly shallow angle of approach to the ball that I need to make solid contact with the blow going forward instead of downward, and I also get the on-path clubhead movement I need to make my shots start out in the right direction.

So far in this chapter I've told you how setting up to the left and sliding laterally puts my clubhead on a rim that moves it down the flight path and into the ball at the right angle of descent. Now let me tell you how I *keep* it moving at ball level a bit longer *past* impact, before it swings upward on the follow-through.

Obviously, it doesn't make any difference where my clubhead is moving once the ball leaves its face. However, the longer I can keep the clubhead moving at ball level, the better I'm protected against catching the ball on the upswing if I have, inadvertently, positioned it too far forward in my stance at address.

All things being equal, keeping my clubhead moving more or less at ball level very far past impact should be an especially big problem for me. Because I align to the left, I must, as I've pointed out, let my left arm leave my left side past impact in order to keep my clubhead from swinging back quickly to the left, where I've aligned. And the sooner this arm leaves my side, the sooner my clubhead *should* start swinging upward. By all rights I should catch a lot of shots on my upswing and either "blade" or top the ball.

But this early upward movement doesn't happen in my swing. In fact, I keep my clubhead moving more or less at ball level for a longer distance past impact than just about any golfer alive. In this respect, I guess, I sort of defy the obvious geometry of the golf swing.

The thing that lets me defy golf geometry—that keeps my club-

90

head moving at ball level instead of flipping upward too soon—is the same thing I told you about in the last chapter when I talked about the importance of making sure that your left hand leads your clubface slightly in the race back to the ball.

The more my left hand leads my clubhead at impact, the farther past impact the clubhead must continue before it finally passes my hand and starts moving upward.

Here again I'm not talking about an extreme difference between what I do and what other golfers do. When my clubhead catches the ball, the back of my left wrist may be bowed outward only a fraction of an inch, but even that fractional difference is enough to give me what amounts to a sizable edge in terms of actual shot results.

As we've seen, it is left-hand control and left-arm acceleration that determines whether the left hand leads the clubhead into the ball. If the right hand takes over, or if the left arm decelerates, you'll cup the back of your left wrist and flip the clubhead upward.

So I'll stress yet again here that you must hold on to the club firmly with the last three fingers of your left hand, to maintain left-hand control, and also slide laterally with your hips and legs, as you start your downswing turn, to set the stage for left-arm acceleration. These are the key factors that will help your clubhead to keep moving forward down your flight path, at ball level, and with its face looking in the right direction a shade longer than it has been.

Now, the more you think about the golf swing, the more you realize that you can overdo anything. It is definitely possible for your hands to win that race back to the ball by *too large* a margin. When that happens, your clubhead probably won't get back to ball level in time, but will catch the top instead of the back of the ball, with the clubface most probably looking out to the right of your flight path.

So, when I talk about left-hand control and acceleration, I'm talking about something most golfers need more of, but I'm also talking about something they can carry to an extreme. Harvey Pennick, an outstanding golf teacher from Austin, Texas, sometimes tells his

HOW TO EXTEND CLUBHEAD
MOVEMENT AT BALL LEVEL

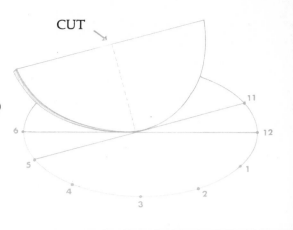

The half-footballs above show the problem of keeping the clubhead moving at ball level longer through impact. The rim of the football in the first drawing shows the clubhead path I could swing along if I set up aligned toward "11 o'clock" for a shot toward "12 o'clock." By cutting this half-football into quarters (second drawing), you see the nice, shallow, down-the-line approach my clubhead makes into the ball when I swing down on the inside rim. The follow-through quarter, however, shows how quickly my clubhead would leave ball level if it continued swinging to my target (third drawing). Below I explain how I eliminate this problem.

The main reason I can keep my clubhead moving low to the ground farther past impact than almost any other golfer is that I make sure that my left hand always beats my clubhead in the race back to the ball. Then, when my clubhead finally does catch up and pass my left hand, well past impact, it's still fairly low to the ground. In short, I've come into the ball shallowly and gone through it shallowly, and thus I've increased my chances of making solid contact when the clubhead is at ball level. To make my left hand beat my clubhead back to the ball, I need plenty of left-arm acceleration (see drawing in the center box) and left-hand control (see drawing in box on right). I can get this acceleration and control only if I grip firmly with the last three fingers of my left hand and start my downswing with the lateral slide to the left (see drawing on far left).

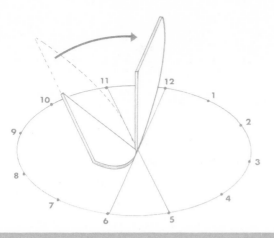

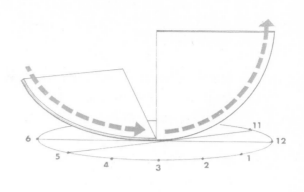

pupils that just because he prescribes an "aspirin" they shouldn't gulp down the whole bottle.

To make sure you don't swallow too many aspirins in trying to build acceleration and left-hand control, I suggest you first ask a friend to check to see if you might be letting your head slide to your left—toward your target—in your downswing. This is a common fault that happens when you think about accelerating your left arm out and down your flight path, especially from an open alignment. It's a trap that I fall into myself occasionally. The head *must* stay back where it was at the start, even while you're sliding laterally to your left with your legs and hips.

Once you're keeping your head steady, try hitting some shots with your feet together—actually touching each other. Hit a few shots this way and see if you make better contact with the ball than you did when your feet were apart. If you do, then you've been getting too *much* body into your downswing and your clubhead is probably trailing too far behind your hands at impact. That means you've got to hit shots with your feet together until you recapture a feeling of rhythm and timing in your swing. Then keep that same feeling of rhythm and timing as you gradually increase your stance to its normal width.

Apart from checking for head movement and hitting some shots with your feet together, which are merely checks against overdoing or misapplying body action, I really haven't told you to do anything new or different in this chapter. All I've really done is explain how the basics of my swing that we've covered before also help me to swing the clubhead at ball level for a slightly longer span through impact.

In other words, you'll get that longer span—and better contact —if you continue to: (1) align yourself and aim your clubface to the left of your flight path at address; (2) start the clubhead back outside that path; (3) shift your weight onto the outside ball of your left foot as you start your downswing turn; (4) maintain control of the club in the last two or three fingers of your left hand; and (5) accelerate your left arm out away from your body and down your flight path past impact.

WHERE TO POSITION THE BALL

The only new elements I'm going to suggest to you in this chapter are ways to find the ideal spot where you should position the ball in relation to your feet.

As I've said before, you can get away with a slight mispositioning of the ball if your clubhead moves down the flight path at ball level and looking in the right direction for a fairly long span through the impact area. You can play the ball, say, an inch or so too far forward, or an inch or so too far back, and still make a pretty good shot. It might not be perfect, but it won't be as bad as it would have been had you not increased those spans.

But you still can't get around the fact that ball position is important. Even if you swing as I do, the span of clubhead movement down the line and at ball level is still a matter of inches. Even in my swing, if I play the ball too far back in my stance—toward my right foot—I can still catch it before my clubhead has started moving down the flight path: when it's still coming from the inside and moving out to the right. When that happens, my clubface also is generally still looking to the right of my flight path, and has not reached ball level. Conversely, if I play the ball too far forward in my stance—too far down my flight path—I may not reach it until my clubhead has started swinging off that path and back to the inside, or has started closing to the left, or has started swinging upward.

When it comes to telling you where to play your ball in your stance, I can't be exact. If I told you exactly where to play it, that might be fine for *you*, but wrong for your wife or son or your favorite golfing partner. Ball position is really something that each golfer has

95

to find for himself. However, here's a simple way to find the position that's best for you.

Start by making a couple of practice swings before you set up to the actual shot. Try to make them the same swing that you'll be trying to make when you're actually at the ball. Align yourself and aim your clubface as you would for the shot at hand, make sure you slide laterally and swing your left arm out and down the flight path, and swing at full power.

After you've made a practice swing, check to see where the clubhead went through the grass. If it swung over the grass instead of through it, or if you cut too deep into the turf, try another practice swing, and maybe even a third, until you get the clubhead moving at the right level through your impact area.

On wood and long-iron shots, you'll want to just barely graze the grass. As you swing the shorter-shafted irons, however, you should be taking a divot from the turf because, the shorter the iron, the closer you'll need to stand to the ball to reach it, and the closer you stand, the more upright your swing plane becomes automatically. This forces your clubhead to make a slightly sharper angle of descent and thus to take a deeper divot.

Once you get the grazing or the cut of turf you're looking for on your practice swing, you'll know pretty much where your clubhead is going to reach ball level on the actual shot. So simply set up to that shot with the ball in the position where the clubhead will catch it without cutting into the turf behind it.

Let's say you've got a wood club in your hand. On your practice swing the clubhead may graze the grass for a span of three or four inches. I suggest you select a spot roughly in the *middle* of that span and then check to see how it relates to where you've placed your feet. The spot might look to be opposite your left heel, or your left toe, or inside your left heel. Wherever it seems to be in relation to your feet is where you should position the ball for your actual shot.

On iron shots, where you want to take a divot, position the ball within your stance according to where your clubhead *entered* the turf on your practice swing.

Once you find the spot where you want to play the ball in your stance, the one other thing to check is where you set your hands. Remember that you want your hands to lead your clubhead slightly through impact, so you might as well start with them in that position.

To ensure this, I suggest that you draw an imaginary line down from the outside of your left shoulder to your clubface when it's set behind the ball. Then make sure that the knuckles of your left hand are pretty much on that line when you play the ball from the spot you've picked out in your stance. You don't need to be exact about this, but try to come close. Check yourself occasionally, just to make sure.

While I'm talking about where to position your ball within the stance, I'd also like to give you a couple of ways to tell how *far* you should stand from the ball. The drill I gave you for checking how far forward or back to play the ball in your stance is also good for telling how far you should be standing from the ball. Merely stand the same distance away from it on your actual shot as your feet were from the marks you made with your clubhead during your practice swing.

Another way to check your distance from the ball is to first set up to a shot at what you think is the right distance from the ball, then have a friend take hold of the club while you let go of it. Finally swing without the club in your hands, making sure you let your right shoulder work under as you swing your left arm out and down your flight path.

As you make this test swing, check how close your right hip comes to the grip end of the club that your friend is holding as you make your downswing turn. If that hip comes closer than two inches to the club as it turns through, then you're standing too close to the ball. Conversely, if you make the proper deep shoulder turn and the right hip passes *more* than two inches from the end of the club, then you'll need to set yourself closer to the ball at address.

97

FINDING HOW FAR TO STAND FROM THE BALL

Here's how I find out if I'm standing the right distance away from the ball. First I set the clubhead on the ground so that it's setting flat on its sole, and then I grip and set up with what feels like a comfortable amount of reaching in my arms. Next I have a friend take hold of the club while I simulate my normal full swing without the club in my hands, making sure I work my right shoulder down and under during the downswing and follow-through. As my hips turn to the left during the forward swing, I check to see how close my right hip comes to the end of the club as it passes by it. If my hip comes less than two inches from the end of the club, I know I've stood too close to the ball

at address. If my hip passes more than two inches from the club, I know I've got to stand closer to the ball on future shots. This two-inch guide applies on any normal shot I want to make.

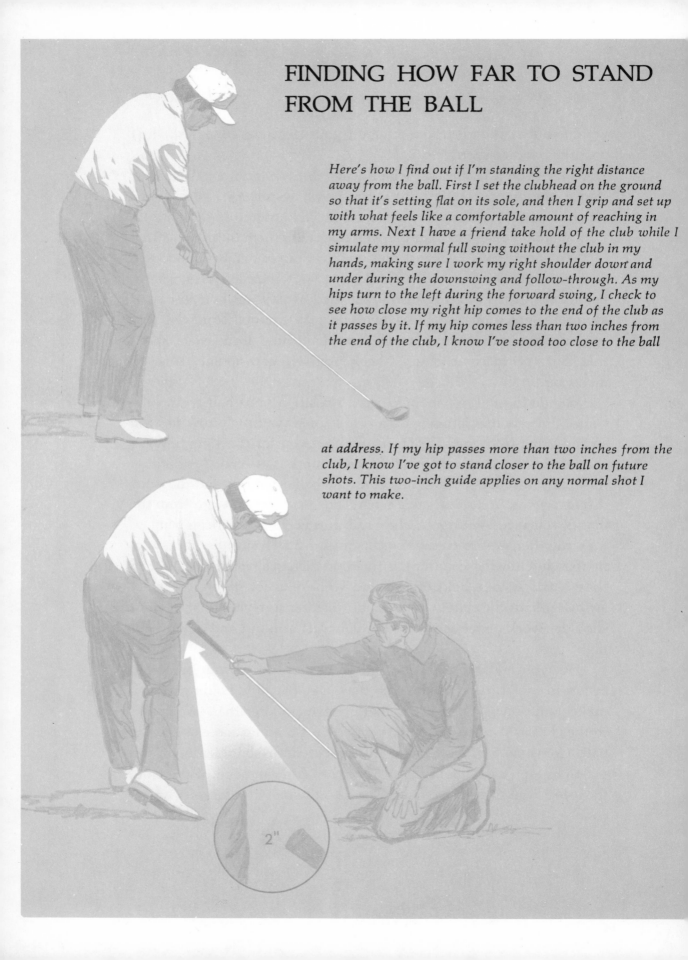

2"

The final points to understand about the distance you stand from the ball are that it won't necessarily be the same for everyone and that it will vary with every club in the bag, because, obviously, you're going to stand closer to the ball with a short-shafted iron club in your hands than you would with a 43-inch driver.

It should also be fairly obvious that a short person with unusually long arms will need to stand farther from the ball than a tall person with relatively short arms. Generally, it follows that the farther a person's fingertips are from the ground when he stands at "attention," the closer he's got to stand to the ball for any given shot, assuming he's using normal-length clubs.

So you can't always measure your distance from the ball along the same lines as another good player, even if he seems to have a physique similar to yours. And you can't expect to stand the same distance from the ball on all your shots. What you can and should do, though, is set up with your hands about the *same distance from your body* on all normal, full shots.

Ball position is something that always seems to need occasional checking. It's all too easy for even the best professionals to slip into bad positioning, which can cause the development of swing compensations that lead to even greater troubles. So I suggest you run the ball-positioning checks I've mentioned here—or at least the one where you make the practice swings—before each round of golf you play, and even on the course if you feel unsure about where to position the ball on any given shot.

4 ADDING—AND CONTROLLING— DISTANCE

HERE COMES THE CHAPTER you've all been waiting for. The topic is *distance,* and for golfers distance is like money; everybody's looking for more—everyone wants a pay raise or a bonus check.

I suppose everyone wants more distance for pretty much the same reasons they want more money. For one thing, a little extra money lets you buy things that you think will add to your esteem—a flashy new car or a fancy wardrobe. Hitting long drives also buys esteem from your fellow golfers, irrespective of what it does for your scores.

Extra money can also mean security and peace of mind, in that it offers some protection against sickness, accident, and other hard times. Extra length from the tee also means security for the golfer, because it takes some of the worry out of his next shot. Most players feel more secure hitting a 6 or 7 iron to the green than they do a 3 or 4 iron, and extra distance off the tee can obviously give them that opportunity.

The only trouble about distance in golf is that most players go after it in all the wrong ways. Instead of being like the man who works hard at a steady job day after day, they're like the guy who seeks his fortune playing the horses or investing in a fly-by-night gold-mine operation. And usually these golfers go broke. They might hit a winner now and then, but generally they play what I call "military golf"—their shots go "left, right, left, right." What's the good of swinging from your heels and snapping your shoestrings on a drive just to put yourself close enough for a 9-iron approach, instead of a 7-iron or 8-iron, if you're going to be playing the 9 iron from the middle of a forest?

When I think of distance in golf, I'm like everyone else because I think about *extra* length. But I also think of distance in another way that maybe you haven't considered. Distance isn't just banging a drive past everyone else in your foursome. One example of what distance really means is hitting the tee shot just far enough to reach a level spot on the fairway. Another—and one club golfers rarely seem to think of—is making approach shots finish fairly close to "hole-high" most of the time, instead of twenty yards short of one green and twenty yards over the next. In short, distance is *control*; distance is *accuracy*. Distance isn't just extra length; it's the right *amount* of length.

While it's true that making the clubhead swing down the flight path a bit longer through impact helps to make my shots start out in the right direction, and while keeping the clubface looking in the right direction a bit longer helps me to curve the ball as I choose, and keeping my clubhead at ball level for a little longer span gives me better contact, I'd probably be pumping gas for a living if my swing didn't allow me to make most of my shots go pretty much the right distance. So in this chapter I'll talk not only about how to get extra distance, and how to make *more* of your shots go as far as your *good* shots now go, but also about how to get the *right amount* of distance for any particular shot.

When golfers talk about distance, the first words that seem to pop out are "clubhead speed." Everyone seems to think that the faster he makes that clubhead travel through impact, the farther he's going to hit the ball. I've often thought that if I could bottle clubhead speed and sell it in pro shops I'd make more money than Mr. Coca-Cola and Mr. Jack Daniel's and Mrs. Chanel No. 5 put together. Well, there's no doubt that extra clubhead speed can add some distance, but by itself it sure isn't any kind of secret elixir. In fact, you can try for an overdose of clubhead speed alone—which is what most golfers do in going for more distance—and end up with one big headache.

The plain truth about clubhead speed is that you can generate enough to drive a golf ball 300 yards and still come up with a weak dribbler just over the front of the tee. Or you can make solid contact and drive the ball 300 yards, but in the wrong direction. Or you can try for clubhead acceleration and actually end up with *less* at impact than you were making earlier in your downswing.

The big point to understand is that clubhead speed doesn't do you any more good than two left shoes if you can't apply it *squarely* to the ball, and if you don't maximize it at the *right moment* in your swing. And the sad thing is that, the faster you try to swing your clubhead, the less chance you have of moving it at top speed at the right time and thus making solid contact.

Distance on golf shots comes from clubhead speed *correctly applied,* and you'll generally apply it correctly more of the time when you don't *try* to apply it at all—when you simply let it happen as a *result* of doing *other things* correctly. These "other things" should all sound quite familiar to you by now, because they're the same things I've been discussing so far in this book.

Please don't be disappointed that I'm not going to sell you some secret medicine for increasing your clubhead speed. I honestly doubt that you need new medicine, because it's my belief that practically every reasonably healthy golfer already has the potential for getting

Here my head is still in position—it hasn't slid to the left—and my right shoulder is working under instead of around. This indicates that I started my downswing turn with a lateral slide of my hips and legs to the left, which dropped my club onto an inside rim for my downswing. My right shoulder would be higher here if I'd used it to shove the club onto an outside rim.

My left arm has just started to move away from my side. I'm still trying to accelerate the arm forward, because if I had let it slow down, my right hand would have taken control of the club. I would not be able to accelerate this arm if I had swung down on an outside rim because my angle of approach to the ball would be too steep. Then proper acceleration would stick the clubhead into the ground behind the ball.

HOW TO GET DISTANCE

To get maximum distance, you need full clubhead speed during impact, plus solid contact. This drawing summarizes the things I'm doing at impact to get this speed and contact. However, each of these elements relates back to my aligning and aiming to the left, my outside-the-path takeaway, my lateral slide, and my left-arm extension on the follow-through.

Here my left wrist is still firm, indicating good left-hand control in the last three fingers. The back of the wrist hasn't cupped inward, which would mean a slowing down of the left arm and an upward flipping of the clubhead with the right hand.

The position of my legs here shows that they, along with my hips, slid laterally to my left as I started my downswing turn. If I'd started down with my shoulders and hands instead, and thus moved my club onto an outside rim, my left leg would be straight and rigid at this point, as I spun around my left side and brought my clubhead across the line from outside to inside during impact.

By now, my clubhead has just passed my left hand, but it's still moving low to the ground—about at ball level—because it trailed that hand during impact. My clubface is still facing down the flight path because of my left-hand control, and its still moving down that path instead of back to the left and around my body.

The position of my feet shows that I shifted my weight from the inside of my right foot onto the outside ball of my left at the start of my downswing turn. If I had instead flipped or shoved my clubhead onto an outside rim at that point, my weight would have stayed on my right foot.

more distance, and for controlling that distance. What he needs is simply a means of getting more out of what he's already got within himself. In other words, it's a matter of correctly applying your present strengths, while cutting down on the mistakes that seem to take over whenever you consciously try to hit a shot into orbit.

SOLID CONTACT

O.K., you need solid contact to get maximum distance. You also need fairly solid contact *consistently* to be able to *control* distance. For example, let's say that on a windless day your 4-iron shots go 170 yards when you connect solidly. But let's say that you make solid contact only once in every five shots with this club, which would be about average for a 10-to-15-handicap golfer. The rest of the time you're usually hitting 4-iron shots, say, 165 to 155 yards, sometimes even less.

Obviously, if you're this golfer and you've got a 170-yard shot to the flagstick, and you pull out your 4 iron, you've got only one chance in five of hitting the shot hole-high. That means *80 percent* of your shots are going to finish short of the hole, or even short of the green.

"That's not me," you say. Well, let's see. Think for a moment about any par-4 hole on your course where you're regularly swinging a long iron—2, 3, or 4—on your approach shot. Ask yourself how many times you've had to chip *back* to the hole from *behind* the green. Then ask yourself how many times you've come up short and had to chip or pitch from in front of the green or putt from the front edge. If you're typical—and honest with yourself—it's my guess that you seldom hit long-iron shots over the green. Most of the time you finish short of the hole.

The reason you've come up short so often is that you've probably chosen the club that you felt would get you to the flagstick if you made *perfectly solid contact*. In other words, you've always tried to make shots that you've actually been able to make only once in a while.

One obvious solution might be to use more club—a 3 iron, say, on a shot where a perfect 4 iron would put you hole-high. Then you could mis-hit the ball—as most golfers do most of the time—and still not come up quite so short of the hole. You might even finish hole-high if you missed the shot just a little bit. But, obviously, if you *did* catch it solidly, you would be chipping or putting from beyond the flagstick.

What all this means is that, regardless of the club you use on any given shot, your chances of hitting that shot the right distance are really no better than your ability to make solid contact. The more frequently you can make solid, or near-solid, contact, the more you can count on your shots going more or less the distance you desire them to go. Even Jack Nicklaus doesn't hit every shot hole-high—I've seen Jack lay it thirty yards short of the hole on a 120-yard wedge shot. But he's usually pretty close to hole-high, because he makes fairly solid contact *most of the time*.

Of course, more frequent solid contact will also give you *more* distance on average. I'd say that most golfers who hit their very best drives 220 yards probably *average* under 200 yards on all drives put together. Thus they've got the potential to increase their *average* drive by twenty or more yards simply by becoming more consistent. And they could hit their average drives that much farther without doing push-ups, drinking carrot juice, or taking Geritol five times a day. All they need to do is make solid contact more often.

How do we increase our percentage of solidly struck shots—and thus our average distance and our distance consistency? I've already answered that question in the earlier chapters. We do it by increasing the span where the clubhead is *moving* in the right direction and *looking* in the right direction while moving more or less at *ball level* through the impact area.

ACCELERATION

Along with solid contact, you need maximum acceleration of the clubhead into the ball if you want to get maximum distance on your shots. Actually, you also need this acceleration to make solid contact, because when your clubhead starts slowing down it's usually going to stop moving down your flight path at ball level while facing in the right direction. I'm sure you've seen this happen whenever you've quit accelerating the clubhead forward on a putt. Usually the putterhead pulls off the line, the face closes to the left or opens to the right, and the putterhead may even scuff the grass.

So acceleration into the ball gives you more distance through added clubhead speed, and it also increases your chances for extra distance by helping to produce a more solid contact. But acceleration does these things only when you go about developing it in the right way.

The golfer who goes after clubhead acceleration in the wrong ways is the golfer who occasionally catches one on the screws and hits it 230 yards, but who usually mis-hits drives 200 yards or less, generally in the wrong direction. He averages maybe 200 yards, but crisscrosses the course like a Bowery drunk on New Year's Eve.

Mainly, there are two *wrong* ways to go about getting clubhead acceleration. One wrong way is with your shoulders; the other is with your hands and wrists. Unfortunately, both are all too instinctive for most of us. We've gotten into the habit of trying to create clubhead momentum by shoving with our shoulders or flicking our hands and wrists because that's how, for example, we've swung a baseball bat, or swept out the garage, or punched out the kid next door.

If you're a golfer who relies mainly on his shoulders for distance, you're actually losing a tremendous amount of clubhead speed.

106

For one thing, the more you labor with your shoulders in your down-swing—since you can't move them very fast—the *slower* you've got to swing your arms. And the slower you swing your arms, the slower your clubhead is going to be moving. What happens, in effect, is that you end up swinging *yourself* instead of the *club*.

Another reason why laboring your shoulders in your down-swing cuts down on clubhead acceleration is that doing so makes you swing back to the ball on the outside rim I talked about in Chapter 1. Excessive shoulder action shoves your clubhead out beyond your flight path prior to impact, so that it must cut back across your flight path—back to the inside—through impact. It's then moving off to the left of where you want your shot to start, as well as chopping down-ward on too steep an angle of attack.

The more your clubhead is swinging off to the left through im-pact, the less you're going to let those arms accelerate the club, because, subconsciously, you can sense that they're going to be accelerating it in the wrong direction. You also won't let them ac-celerate as fully as they might because you're chopping downward, instead of swinging forward with the clubhead, and you don't want to stick it into the ground and sprain a wrist.

So going for distance with your shoulders can actually cost you clubhead speed. So can going for distance with your hands and wrists, and for several similar reasons.

First, when you flip the club with your hands and wrists from the top of the backswing, you can easily flip it out and onto the same outside rim you'd be swinging along if you labored your shoulders. Again, this leads subconsciously to deceleration, because you know you don't want to flip the clubhead off to the left or deep into the ground. Most "flippy" golfers avoid doing so by lifting up their bodies and falling back on their right foot and opening the clubface to the right at impact, the result being a lot of slices that start left and curve right, especially with the woods and long irons. Of course, they

107

lose even more momentum by the falling-back action, not to mention lack of solid contact caused by the clubhead starting upward before it reaches the ball.

Going for distance with your hands and wrists can also make you lose clubhead speed too soon because your right hand takes over and breaks down the firmness in your left wrist. This does create acceleration by throwing the clubhead forward, but too often this maximum acceleration happens too soon—*before* the clubhead reaches the ball.

If you could time your swing perfectly so that you neither flipped the clubhead closed too soon nor threw it onto the outside rim, you could get some extra distance with a very wristy swing (which is how many of the great old golfers played). But all this takes perfect timing, and a great sense of rhythm and pace, and few weekend golfers can be that perfect very often, especially under pressure or when faced with a difficult shot.

The right way to get good distance consistently through acceleration and solid contact is to make a full shoulder and body turn on your backswing, and then rely on your legs and arms instead of your shoulders and hands. What it amounts to in the final analysis is that, the more you can accelerate your left arm down your flight path through impact, the more clubhead acceleration you'll get. And the way to get this arm acceleration is to start your downswing turn with a lateral sliding of your hips and legs, instead of a shoving with your shoulders or flipping with your hands. It's my belief that any normal person can learn to make a good lateral hip slide at the start of the downswing turn, but that no one can do this if he doesn't give himself enough *time* to let the hips and legs move first. Anytime you swing up and down too fast—or even up slowly and then down too fast—your hands and wrists, or your shoulders, are going to jump the gun ahead of your hips and legs.

Jack Nicklaus says that he found one of the most difficult things in golf was to discipline himself against flashing his hands and wrists out and down from the top of his backswing. He also says that when he wants to drive the ball extra distance, he consciously *slows down* the pace of his backswing. In other words, Jack and I agree that you've got to give yourself *time* at the changeover from backswing to downswing to let your hips, legs, and arms do the leading.

One point I should stress again here is that it is much more difficult to achieve effective lateral sliding and strong arm acceleration from a square or closed address position than from an open position. For anatomical rather than golfing reasons, the left side must clear out of the way—turn to the left—to make room for the left arm to swing freely through the impact area. By aligning yourself to the left in an open address position, you preset yourself so that your left side is already partly turned to the left, which is where you want it to move *to* in the downswing.

By preturning this side to the left at address, I can still make a full backswing turn to the right and slide laterally as I turn back to the left on my downswing, yet still clear my left side out of the way to make room for my left arm to accelerate in the proper direction, which is down my flight path. I get left-arm acceleration—for maximum clubhead speed—and the right angle of clubhead approach into the ball—for solid contact—because I'm on the inside rim. So I also can put more force into the blow because, by sliding laterally, I'm also applying the big muscles of my legs and back.

If you align yourself in the standard square position at address, with everything parallel to the flight path, then it takes a lot more physical effort to get your left hip out of the way so that your left arm can accelerate in the proper direction during your downswing. In fact, the more you align to the right at address in a closed stance, the more difficult this clearing of the left side becomes.

I've found, in the last several years, that more and more of the touring professionals are setting up to their shots aligned more and more to the left of their flight path, though still not to the extreme that I do. This, of course, allows them to clear the left hip *and* make

109

the lateral slide that drops the club onto an inside rim, which, in turn, allows maximum arm and club acceleration into the ball. The fact that these great players, with tons of natural talent and years of practice behind them, are tending more and more to set up in a way that makes it easier for them to clear the left hip makes me believe that mine is no bad way to play golf, different as it may seem at first.

On the other hand, we're still teaching *less skilled* players to set up parallel to their flight path: to align in a way that demands *more* ability, more talent for hip clearing. And then we wonder why so many pupils continually fail to turn through the shot properly. We wonder why, instead, they keep shoving the club onto an outside rim with their shoulders, from where they've got no chance to accelerate their arms and clubhead into the ball.

I'm not saying that aligning to the left is the answer for everyone who's trying to increase his clubhead speed—in the next chapter I'll point out some pitfalls that can result if you set up to the left but don't do the other things I've suggested. But, at the very least, aligning to the left gives you a *chance* to accelerate your arms in the right direction, and a *chance* to build some extra power from using your legs, and thus to apply the clubhead to the ball as squarely and as fast as possible in terms of your own dexterity and physical condition.

DISTANCE CONTROL

One nice thing about my method of playing golf is that you use the same parts of your body to *control* distance as you use to *increase* distance. I've stressed that you should rely on your lower body—hips and legs—and left-arm acceleration to make your full shots fly farther with greater consistency. I've shown how relying on your shoulders reduces acceleration and solid contact.

To *control* distance, I use my hips and legs to control the speed at which I accelerate my left arm and, thus, the clubhead. I say "hips

LET HIPS AND LEGS CONTROL YOUR LENGTH

On all normal, full shots I think of my hips and legs as being the big wheel that controls the speed of the progressively smaller wheels—my arms, wrists and, finally, the club itself. The farther I want to hit a shot with any given club, the faster I slide my hips and legs laterally to the left as I start my downswing turn. The faster I slide, the faster I can—and must—accelerate my arms and then the club through impact. Even when I'm trying for less than normal distance, however—and even on a putt— I still want some *arm and club acceleration into the ball.*

and legs" because I work them pretty much as a unit. I do *think* more about my left hip, though, when it comes to setting the pace for my downswing.

I like to think that my left hip is the big wheel in my swing mechanism. Its speed of movement is what controls the speed of the smaller wheels—my arms, wrists, hands, and, finally, the clubhead itself. If I happen to be standing on the tee of a hole where I've got plenty of open fairway, and I figure I can let out a little extra shaft, I just think about sliding that left hip laterally to the left a little bit faster than normal as I start my downswing turn. That faster hip movement makes all the little wheels work a little faster in sequence, the result being a few extra yards.

On the other hand, if I've got a wedge shot of say 80 to 90 yards, which doesn't require a full-power swing, then I simply slide the left hip a little more *gradually* to the left. Then, although I'll still try to accelerate my left arm down and out along the flight path, I'll get a little less acceleration because of slowing down the hip slide.

By controlling my distance with the speed of my hip slide, I can take a dozen balls, stand 90 yards from my target, and, given no wind and a good lie, make them all carry between 88 and 92 yards. If I tried the same thing controlling the length of the shots with, say, my hands and wrists, there's no way I could do nearly as well, especially if there was something riding on my performance. My hands and wrists—those little "wheels"—would be sure to "choke" sooner or later. And the slightest grabbing with my hands would make me mis-hit the shot or strike it solidly but too far. The best way I know to keep from choking with my hands and wrists is to concentrate solely on moving that left hip, simply letting my hands and wrists *react* to that movement, instead of trying to make them act on their own.

Now, before I close this chapter on increasing and controlling distance, I'd like to leave you with one last tip. I think you should try to swing with no more than 80 to 90 percent of your maximum physical resources on most full shots, for the simple reason that when you swing "within yourself" to that extent, you'll do a much better job of timing and coordinating the various components of the action. You'll give yourself the time you need to let your hips and legs lead your downswing, instead of your hands and wrists or your shoulders. And you'll also start to develop a feel for controlling distance with the movement of your left hip.

If you are like most golfers, you may be using far too *little* effort in your *practice* swings, and far too *much* effort in the swings that *count*. I suggest you reverse that process. The next time you take a practice swing, give it 120 percent effort—really let it all hang out. Then, on your actual shot, cut back to 80 or 90 percent. You may just find that this alone immediately gives you more distance by allowing you to strike the ball more squarely through better timing.

5 PUTTING IT ALL TOGETHER

U P T O N O W I've discussed in separate chapters the four impact factors—clubhead path, clubhead facing, clubhead level, and clubhead speed—that determine the success or failure of all golf shots. In this chapter we're going to put all these elements into a single perspective, so that you'll be able to do a better job of applying them *consistently*—so that you will *react* correctly on swing after swing. At this point, I also want to warn you about some things you must *not* do if you hope to make my system work.

Let's start by imagining you've gone to the grocery store because you decided you'd like a nice cantaloupe for tomorrow's breakfast. You get to the fruit department and you find a big selection of cantaloupes, but, because they all look quite eatable, you're not sure which one to buy. So you test a few. You pinch them, thump them, smell them. Finally you find the one you think is best, and you carry it away hoping it will be ripe and sweet inside, instead of underripe and tasteless or overripe and rotten. You've made a decision, but you'll never know if it was correct until you actually taste the melon.

Playing golf is just like buying cantaloupe. Before you swing,

114

you do everything you can to ensure a good shot, but you never know for sure if you've done the right things, or if you've made the right swing, until the ball is on its way.

The reason you can't be sure about any shot longer than a six-inch putt is that golf is a game of *reflex reactions*. In golf you might not be reacting to a pitch, as in baseball, or a serve, as in tennis, but you *do* react to a multitude of other factors on every swing you make.

You might, for instance, react to something you feel—a strong wind in your face, perhaps, which might make you instinctively try to swing harder than normal, to make up for the loss of distance you expect the headwind to cost you. Swinging harder into the wind would be a normal human reflex reaction, but almost always a bad one so far as golf is concerned.

Or you might react to something you see, such as out-of-bounds down the left side of the fairway. This might make you reflexively aim and swing out to the right, or it might make you open your club-face to the right just before impact.

Or you might react to something you hear, such as the opinion of someone who's just come up short on a putt ("These greens sure are slow today").

Or you might react to something you've done before, such as— if you've been slicing your shots—swinging the clubhead back to the left of target on the downswing, which could make you slice even more. In short, there are scores of factors to react to in golf, from the lie of the ball in the grass, to the slant of the fairway in front of you, to the tackiness, or slipperiness, of the grip on your club.

All these things that I've said that you might react to are things that are present *before* you swing the club. The experienced golfer knows how to react to such situations in a way that's good for him, by making whatever adjustment is necessary *before* he swings. If he's playing in wind, for instance, he might choke down on his club a little, to make it easier to control and to keep himself from over-swinging. If his opponent comes up short on a putt, he might first

115

decide if the greens are really all that slow, or if the other golfer simply mis-hit the ball.

Sometimes even good golfers don't do enough pre-shot planning to guarantee a good swing. They might overlook an important factor altogether, or they might make the wrong adjustment.

Other times you react *during* your swing to something that happened *after* you had already started swinging. For example, you might get to the top of the backswing and sense that you're going to slice the shot to the right, and react by flipping or rolling your clubface off to the left in the downswing. Or you might sense you're going to hook to the left, and react by opening the clubface to the right. Or in your downswing you might sense that your clubhead is going to cut too far under the ball, and instinctively lift your body at the last split second—or you might sense that you're going to top the ball and instinctively dip downward.

The point I want to make is that we all *react* when we're swinging a golf club because there are so many factors around us to react to. Sometimes we react the right way, sometimes we don't. Sometimes we react the right way but to the wrong degree—and over-reacting the right way can sometimes be worse than reacting the wrong way.

Now, obviously, we can't eliminate all the factors that make us react: can't stop the wind from blowing, or play from out-of-bounds areas, or gag other people. What we can do, however, is try to make ourselves react properly in order to ensure so far as possible that any adjustment we do make as we swing is the correct adjustment, or at least a *predictable* adjustment. Ideally, you would develop a swing in which you react the *same* way and the *right* way on most of your shots. The next-best thing is to react the *same* way on most shots, even if it isn't quite the right way. Then, although you might not make a perfect shot, at least you'll know what to expect: you can at least plan the shot that will compensate for the imperfection you know is coming.

The least desirable way to play golf is to react *differently* from shot to shot, even if you occasionally react perfectly and make a super shot. That once-in-a-blue-moon shot might be a thing of beauty that you'd want to frame and hang over your mantel, but the rest of the time you're going to find golf extremely frustrating and embarrassing—sometimes even physically painful.

I think that the main reason why the old system of swinging a golf club hasn't worked for most golfers is that it allows too many different reactions. Because the choice of reactions is so wide and varied with the so-called orthodox way of swinging a club, it's very easy to make a reaction that you didn't expect to make—it's like choosing the right cantaloupe from a big selection in which all of them look about the same.

I think my own system of swinging is better because it offers only one obviously eatable cantaloupe—all the others are obviously rotten. My system makes it easy to react the same way each time you swing—to buy the best cantaloupe—because any other reaction would obviously be rotten and distasteful.

Fortunately, my system not only *forces* you to make the same correct reaction each time, but also *allows* you to make it. It forces—and allows—you to swing in a way so that, at impact, your clubhead is: (1) moving down the flight path, (2) more or less at ball level, (3) facing in the right direction, at (4) pretty close to the proper speed for the length of the shot.

Now, here are the procedures I suggest you follow and the things that my system both *demands* and *allows* you to do. You'll find these procedures produce a chain reaction from start to finish that is designed to make your shots more consistent.

1. Pick your target and visualize the shot you want to make—and realistically think you *can* make—under the existing conditions. These conditions will include such factors as the lie of the ball, the direction and strength of the wind, and the terrain and any obstacles between the ball and the target. Be very realistic at this point: don't

plan a shot you don't think you can make on most of your tries, unless the status of a match absolutely demands that you go for broke.

2. Select the club that you feel will best allow you to make the shot you've visualized. If you're not making solid contact reasonably consistently, keep in mind that by using more club than you may seem to need—say a 4 iron instead of a 5 iron—you'll probably make a smoother, better controlled swing. And also that, even if you still mis-hit the ball slightly, the stronger club may keep your shot from finishing in trouble short of the green.

3. If you're undecided about where to play the ball in your stance, or if you feel physically "tight," take a practice swing or two to loosen up and find out where your clubhead is going to catch or graze the turf. Then position yourself to your ball accordingly. Remember also that if you apply *more* than normal effort on your practice swings, you'll be more likely to *react* with *proper* effort during your actual stroke. Using too *little* effort on practice swings generally makes most people *react* with too *much* effort on the actual stroke.

4. Grip the club with the back of your left hand aligned with the leading edge of your clubface, because this alignment will give you more *direct* control over where your clubhead faces as you swing.

5. As you assume your grip, sense that you are controlling the club largely with the last three fingers of your left hand. This will help program you beforehand for the left-hand control needed later on to keep the clubface looking in the right direction and moving at ball level through impact.

6. Set the clubface behind the ball. As you do, keep in mind the flight of the shot you've visualized making. Aim your clubface and align yourself to the left of where you want the ball to start its flight. The degree to which you aim and align to the left should be determined by the "shape" of the shot you have visualized.

Aiming and aligning to the left will force you to *react* by swinging your left arm out and down your flight path through impact. The reactions that aiming and aligning to the left *disallow* are swinging the clubhead back off to the left, or turning the clubface off to the left. In either case, you'd be buying a rotten cantaloupe, because your ball would start out *and* curve to the left.

7. Start your backswing with your clubhead moving *outside* your initial flight path, or in other words parallel to your body alignment. Starting the clubhead back outside the flight path *demands* that you *react* correctly by making a full backswing turn to set your club in position so that later you can swing it back to the ball from *inside* to along your flight path. But if you don't turn fully you'll get a bad cantaloupe for sure—a clubhead moving down from outside that path and cutting off to the left through impact.

What you must never, *never* do is align to the left and then start the clubhead back from the ball either along or inside the flight path. If you make that sort of takeaway—along an inside rim—on the backswing, you'll almost certainly *react* by throwing or shoving the club back onto the outside rim at the start of the downswing. Then you've got a dozen rotten cantaloupes on your hands.

8. Slide your left hip and legs laterally to the left as you start your downswing turn. You should feel as if you're shifting your weight from the inside of your right foot toward the outside ball of your left foot.

While aligning to the left at address has *allowed* you to *react* by making the outside-the-path takeaway, that takeaway has demanded that you *react* by sliding laterally to drop the club onto the inside rim. The open alignment is what *allows* you to clear your left side out of the way as you make the lateral slide.

Remember that you *must* give yourself enough *time* at the transition from backswing to downswing for your hips and legs to lead the action. Also, you must hold your head steady as you slide laterally—don't under any circumstances let it shift to the left as you slide in that direction.

9. Accelerate your left arm as you swing the clubhead down to the ball and out along your flight path. To do this you must keep your

DOS AND DON'TS

My method is designed to build consistency into your game by forcing you to react the same way during each swing. It forces you to react the same way by putting you on the brink of disaster, so that only the correct reactions will save you from making a disastrous shot. At the same time, the ingredients of my method allow the correct set of reactions. I set myself on the brink of disaster from the start by aligning myself and aiming my club to the left of my flight path, as shown below. The correct and incorrect reactions that should and should not result from this address position are shown in the drawings on the right.

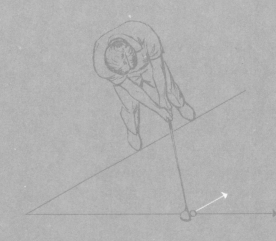

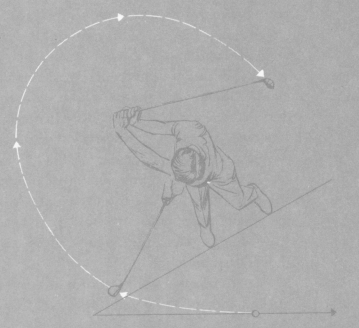

YOU MUST *start the clubhead back slightly outside your flight path and then swing it up and around your body with a full hip and shoulder turn. Aligning to the left at address makes this easy to do.*

YOU MUST NOT *start the clubhead back immediately inside your flight path. This "bad cantaloupe" could make you fan the clubface too open, swing your arms on too flat a plane, and program you to return the club onto an outside rim during the downswing.*

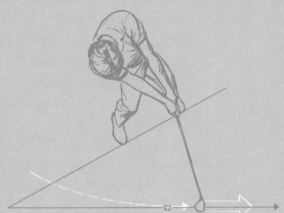

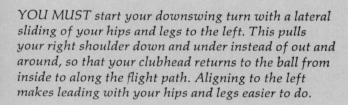

YOU MUST start your downswing turn with a lateral sliding of your hips and legs to the left. This pulls your right shoulder down and under instead of out and around, so that your clubhead returns to the ball from inside to along the flight path. Aligning to the left makes leading with your hips and legs easier to do.

YOU MUST let your left arm leave your side as you swing through the ball, so that the clubhead moves down the flight path for a long enough span to guarantee that your shots will start out in the right direction—even if your timing or your ball-positioning wasn't perfect.

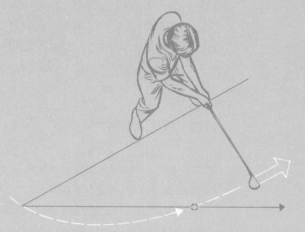

YOU MUST NOT start your downswing with your shoulders or your hands and wrists, which would shove or throw the clubhead onto an outside rim. Then it would move through the ball on a path that's far to the left of your initial flight path, in the direction in which you aligned yourself and aimed the club at address.

YOU MUST NOT spin off to the left or keep your left arm tight to your side as you swing through the ball. This would make your shots start disastrously far to the left, since, again, you've set up and aimed your clubface to the left at address.

flight path in mind throughout your swing. The lateral slide *allows* you to *react* by accelerating your left arm, and this acceleration helps to *allow* you to maintain left-hand control, which *allows* you to face your clubhead in the right direction longer, and swing it at ball level longer, through the impact area.

It all boils down to a few "do's":

—*Do* visualize your shot beforehand and carefully select your initial flight path.

—*Do* keep your flight path in mind both as you set up to the shot and throughout your swing.

—*Do* hold the club with the back of your left hand and your clubface aligned.

—*Do* establish control of the club largely in the last two or three fingers of your left hand, and maintain this control through impact.

—*Do* aim the clubface to the left of your flight path, the degree depending on how much you want the shot to curve.

—*Do* align your stance and your body left of your flight path according to how you want the shot to curve.

—*Do* start the clubhead back *outside* your flight path, or parallel to your body alignment.

—*Do* slide your left hip and legs laterally to the left as you start your downswing turn, and give yourself time for this to happen.

—*Do* accelerate your left arm and clubhead out and down your flight path through impact and slightly beyond.

—*Do* keep your head steady throughout your swing.

HELPFUL HINTS

Here are a few things that I've found help make my system work better for me and for others.

First, I plan everything about my shot *before* I step into my address position. This lets me "pull the trigger" sooner, before I have a chance to build up a lot of mental or physical tension.

Second, once I'm over the ball I always keep something moving before I actually start my swing. I'm waggling the club with the last three fingers of my left hand, just to alert them that they will be controlling the club in my swing. I'm moving my legs a little bit, "pumping them up" so to speak, to let them know they've got a job to do at the start of my downswing.

Third, with my left hand still in control and my head steady, I stretch my left arm out as far as I possibly can during my backswing, as I turn fully to swing the club back and up and around behind me. This gets all my muscles working and stretching to build maximum power. It also gives me the *time* I need to allow my legs and hips to silde laterally as the first move of my downswing.

If you have any trouble making my system work in your practice sessions, these three helpful hints should put you back on track, so long as you're following all the "do's" I just listed.

6 FINESSING FROM TROUBLE—AND ELSEWHERE

A FEW YEARS AGO I was playing quite well in the Thunderbird Open at Upper Montclair, New Jersey, when I came to the twelfth hole with a little lake on the left side of the fairway. There I cut my tee shot a bit too much and the ball finished just on the edge of the water. Since the ball didn't look too submerged, I went in and tried to splash it out. I tried to contact the ball just as I would on a normal shot, but it didn't come out. So I tried again. It still didn't come out. On my third swing I managed to move the ball a little bit—into even deeper water.

By then I was cussin' and fumin' pretty good, because if I'd simply dropped out in the first place and taken the one-stroke penalty, I could have made an easy bogey on the hole. But here I was dropping back on the far side of the water and getting ready to play my sixth stroke. I was so hot that I drilled that shot into the water too.

I won't drag this on any further, except to say that this particular hole was very close to the parking lot. After I'd rung up something like twelve or fourteen strokes, I simply grabbed my bag, paid off my caddie, hopped in my car, and headed out of town. Jesse James never made a faster getaway.

I'm telling you this story because this chapter is about how to play special types of shots, including the one from water. Since that episode in the Thunderbird, I've learned something about playing from ponds and streams, and a lot of other places I hope you'll see much less of in the future, once you've developed the swing pattern I've talked about in this book.

SHOTS FROM WATER

I'll start with the water shot, not because it's one that you'll need very often, but because I've already started you thinking about it.

The reason I made that big score in the Thunderbird was that I tried to play the shot from the water in the same way I play iron shots from the fairway, where I contact the ball before it cuts down into the turf. This technique didn't work in the water because my clubhead couldn't penetrate it deep enough to reach the ball.

The thing I didn't know at the time was that the way to play this shot is to make your clubhead hit the water two or three inches *behind* the ball. That way, the force of the contact makes the ball jump up in the water, so that your clubhead can catch it without having to cut so deeply. Obviously you can't hit the ball very far because the water slows down your clubhead so much, but you can generally at least get it out. Most people can make this shot work if the ball is submerged only an inch or so under the surface of the water. If it's any lower than that, you'd better settle for dropping out and accepting the penalty stroke.

I'd also like to warn you about playing these shots barefoot. It might seem silly to wade in with your golf shoes on, but I've seen too many golfers cut their feet on glass, tin cans, or rocks. It's far better to take a penalty, or even play the rest of the round in a wet shoe, than to cut yourself badly and miss out on your golfing for several weeks.

HITTING HIGH SHOTS AND LONG IRONS

Since I play my shots with the longer-shafted iron clubs—the 1, 2, 3, and 4 irons—the same way I play shots that I want to hit extra high with other clubs, I'll discuss both subjects together.

In the old days it wasn't so important to hit long-iron shots high. The hard, unwatered greens wouldn't hold them anyway, and there was less sand and water blocking the path of low run-up shots than we find on modern courses.

Today, however, it is a big advantage to be able to hit the long approach shots high, to fly those hazards and plop the ball down on the lush, watered greens that will hold almost any high-flying shot.

One way to put some extra height on your long-iron shots is to simply play the ball a shade farther forward in your stance, say opposite the middle of your left foot instead of off your left heel. This simple adjustment can work if you don't carry the forward placement to an extreme, and if you keep your left arm accelerating forward through impact. Moving the ball too far forward—I'd say more than an inch—might cause you to catch it on the upswing, and thus lose some of the backspin that you need to make the ball rise. The same thing might happen if your left arm slows down and gives your right hand a chance to flip the clubhead upward.

So, if you want more height on these shots, I suggest you first try playing the ball a bit farther forward in your stance, but if you start digging your clubhead into the ground behind it, or if you start catching it thin or topping it, then you'd better go back to your original ball position and try my next suggestion.

That suggestion is to start "hooding" your clubface slightly at address. By "hooding" I mean taking some loft off the clubface by aiming it a bit farther to the *left* than normal as you set up to the shot.

Why take loft off the club at address to make the ball fly higher

126

in the air? Well, it all goes back to my "brink of disaster" theory. Let's say you set up with your clubface turned to the *right* of your flight path, which would *seem* logical if you wanted to hit higher shots, because the turning of the club to the right adds a few degrees of loft to its face.

The problem is that aiming to the right can make you react with an extreme rolling of your wrists to the left as you swing back to the ball, to avoid hitting the shot to the right where you've aimed the club in the first place. Too much rolling of the wrists then turns the clubface closed to the left and reduces the loft it carries during impact.

Aiming left and hooding the clubface at address triggers the opposite reaction. You resist rolling your wrists to the left because that would certainly be a bad cantaloupe, since you've already aimed to the left. Instead of "closing the gate" by rolling your wrists to the left, you'll now instinctively hold the clubface open a bit through impact, which gives you the extra loft you need to make the ball fly higher. This adjustment also gives you more left-hand control, because that's what you need to keep the gate open.

I always had trouble getting my long irons to fly high until I hit on the idea of aiming more to the left at address, as I've just described. Another thing that helped me hit these shots higher was something that Sam Snead suggested at the 1968 U.S. Open in Rochester, New York. Sam told me to make sure I kept my head and shoulders back as I swung down and through the ball. I'd been letting my upper body slide forward toward the target—to my left—and the more I slid to the left, the more I was, in effect, playing the ball back to the right in my stance, which took loft off the clubface. So if you do hit your shots unusually low, first ask someone to check that you're not sliding your head and shoulders forward during your downswing.

Finally, I've got to tell you that the only way to develop higher shots, especially with the longer irons, is to practice with these clubs. Neglecting the long irons in your practice sessions only lessens your

HOW I FLY MY LONG IRONS HIGH

To make my long irons fly high enough to hold the greens upon landing, I play the ball slightly farther forward in my stance and aim my clubface a little more to the left. Playing the ball forward lets me catch it a bit later in my swing, when my clubhead is moving forward instead of downward. Aiming more left forces me to avoid hitting left by swinging back to the ball on an inside rim instead of chopping down to it on an outside rim. The fear of hitting left also forces me to hold firm with my left hand so that I won't let my wrists roll to the left through impact. The less I roll my wrists the more loft I have on the clubface when it meets the ball.

HOW I FLY MY SHORT IRONS LOW

I like to hit my shorter-iron shots fairly low, so they stay out of any wind, but with enough backspin to settle quickly on the green. I achieve the lower shot and the backspin by playing the ball a little farther back than normal in my stance—more toward my right foot. The trick on these shots is to hit them both low and straight. Too often you play the ball back and then catch it before the clubface has a chance to square itself, when it's still looking off to the right. I make sure I get my clubface back to square at impact by aligning myself and aiming my clubface slightly less to the left than normally. Then I try to swing my arms down to the ball without turning my hips as far to the left as usual. Swinging down freely with my arms ahead of my hips causes my arms and hands to square my clubface a little sooner than they normally would, so that the shot goes straight instead of off to the right.

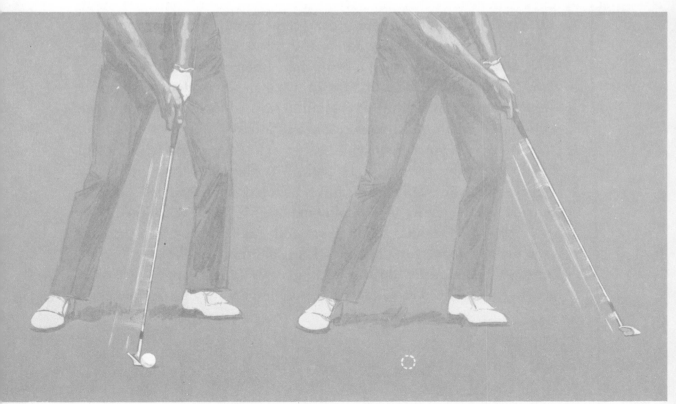

confidence in them, and lack of confidence in a particular club is the surest thing I know for ruining your chances to play good shots with it.

HITTING LOW SHOTS AND SHORT IRONS

Again I'm grouping two categories together—hitting shots lower than normal and playing the shorter iron clubs (7, 8, and 9 irons and the wedges)—because my technique is the same in each case and because so many golfers need less height with these more lofted clubs. If, however, you happen to be someone who needs *more* height on your short irons, then you should study what I've just said about hitting shots higher.

Almost anyone can hit a low shot, but what takes some doing is to hit the ball lower than normal and still fairly straight. It's a shot I love to play, because, generally I kill 'em with it.

To make this shot I first set up with the ball positioned farther back in my stance than normal. If I really want to drill one quail-high, I'll actually play it back opposite my right foot. Playing the ball back in my stance, but with my hands still forward in their normal position, obviously takes some loft off the clubface right at the start.

Now, playing the ball back in my stance to keep the shot low would normally make hitting it straight fairly difficult, because, when you play the ball back, your clubhead naturally returns to it earlier than normal in your downswing, when it's still moving (and facing) out to the right of your flight path. The shot flies low, but to the right, unless you overcompensate and chop down to the ball along an outside rim, when the shot would tend to go low and to the left.

What I do to hit straight shots with the ball back in my stance is to make a downswing in which I feel that my arms are *leading* my hips. When my arms do the leading, two things happen: (1) they return my clubhead to ball level sooner, and (2) they square my club-

130

face sooner. These two adjustments give me solid contact and straight shots, even though I've played the ball back in my stance to make it fly low.

I also stand a bit closer to the ball than normal for this shot, which sets my hands slightly closer to my body and really forces me to swing my arms down ahead of my hips. If I don't—if my right hip swings around too soon—it will force my arms to swing my clubhead out beyond the ball.

So, to summarize how I play my short-iron shots and others I want to hit extra low: I play the ball back in my stance; stand slightly closer to it than normal, and then swing my arms freely down and through with a slightly later hip turn to the left.

HOOKING ON PURPOSE

To me, hooking the ball on purpose is like going out on a blind date; it's something you do only when you're desperate, because you can't be sure what you're going to end up with. It's not the most dependable shot around, because to make it happen you've got to really roll your hands and wrists to the left through impact, and, as I've said, you never know for sure how these fast-moving parts of your anatomy are going to perform.

I think the average golfer is better off if he doesn't consciously try to roll his wrists to the left, but instead sets himself up at address so that they are forced to roll on their own. That means aligning yourself and aiming your clubface less to the left than normal, or even slightly to the right of your flight path. You'll feel like you're set up to hit the shot to the right, but if you swing your arms down freely along the inside rim, your arms, wrists, and hands should react by rolling the clubface closed, into a hooking position, by impact.

If you find that you still don't hook this shot, even after aligning and aiming to the right, then grip the club with your right hand a bit

131

more under the shaft so that your palm is facing somewhat more upward and less forward. This puts the right hand into a stronger position for rolling the clubface to the left during your downswing.

Again, this is a shot that you should work on during your practice sessions. Only a fool tries any of these offbeat shots on the course without having first made them successfully many times in practice. If you watch Jack Nicklaus or Lee Trevino practicing before a tournament round, you'll see us bending shots all over the place in every imaginable direction. All we're doing is finding out just how much curve we can expect to be able to control once we're on the course that particular day.

SLICING ON PURPOSE

I suspect that this section will be the least read portion of this book. Most golfers need less, not more, ability to slice shots from left to right.

For the minority who need help in slicing, however, I suggest aiming the clubface and aligning yourself more to the left of your initial flight path than normal during your swing, while holding on to the club even tighter than normal with the last three fingers of your left hand to make sure that your left hand beats the clubhead in the race back to the ball.

LONG THUMB VERSUS SHORT THUMB

While I'm talking about intentionally curving shots to the left or right, I might as well mention that the distance you extend your left thumb down the shaft as you grip the club can radically change the "shape" of your shots.

132

I once asked Tom Weiskopf why he extends his left thumb so far down the clubshaft. His exact words were: "Baby, when you use that 'long thumb,' you're never gonna hook a shot." I tried it, and sure enough I didn't hook—I left the shot about 100 yards out to the right!

The farther you extend the left thumb down the shaft, the tighter it forces the last three fingers of that hand to grip the shaft. That gives you more left-hand control and a firmer left wrist, and these are factors that keep you from throwing the clubface into a hooking position with your right hand.

I wouldn't advise using an extremely long thumb unless you're going through a really bad siege of hooking. However, you might find that a slightly longer left thumb than you are now using may quickly give you more left-hand control. And that little extra control might be all you need to keep your clubface looking in the right direction a little longer through impact.

Since most right-handed golfers need more left-hand control— or less right-hand control—relatively few golfers should play with an extremely short left thumb. I feel the short thumb allows too much right-hand influence and, personally, I rely on my right hand for eating, but not very much for golfing.

SHOOTING IN THE WIND

What most golfers do when the wind is blowing in their faces is swing harder than normal. I suppose this is a natural reaction, but it's all wrong. The harder you swing, the more spin you put on the ball, and the headwind will accentuate the effect of that spin even more than normal. The more the ball is backspinning, the higher it will fly, and who needs high shots into a strong headwind? The more it's sidespinning, the more it will curve sideways. When it comes to turning a ten-yard fade into a thirty-yard slice, a strong headwind works quicker than an overdose of Ex-Lax.

The next time you're hitting into a headwind or a strong crosswind, take an even longer and less lofted club than you think you need. Then choke down on the shaft an inch or so and swing *easier* than normal. You'll maintain better balance, make better contact, and the less lofted club will fly your shot lower, under the wind.

Along with that advice, you might also want to follow the suggestions I've just made on hitting shots lower than normal: play the ball back in your stance; stand a bit closer to it; and accelerate your arms—but not your hips—freely through impact.

Playing shots with the wind calls for different tactics, since a following wind tends to reduce the ball's spin and thus makes shots fly a bit straighter but lower than normal. Therefore, on downwind approach shots, simply choose a club with more loft than you'd expect to use. A really good golfer might get away with swinging a bit more forcefully on downwind shots, but I don't think most players should give in to that temptation. A lot of wind, even when it's with you, can throw you off balance, especially if you're overswinging.

SWINGING IN THE RAIN

In all honesty, when it comes to playing shots in wet weather I'll have to bow to the Nicklauses and Millers, who learned their golf on lush courses up North. These players have mastered the knack of skimming the ball cleanly from atop soggy turf. Taking deep divots from mushy soil is like hitting out of mashed potatoes; the ball goes nowhere.

I've found that the best way to play these shots, especially with the irons, is to choose more club than you need for the distance—say a 6 iron instead of a 7 iron—choke down on the shaft an inch or so, and then swing a little easier than normal. Choking down helps you contact the ball cleanly instead of cutting under it, the smoother swing helps you keep your balance on the wet grass, and the stronger club compensates for the distance you lose by choking down and swinging easier.

And don't forget that, should you happen to find your ball sitting in a temporary accumulation of water, or if you yourself need to stand in temporary water to make your swing, you are entitled to a free drop. Just lift the ball and drop it over your shoulder at a spot within two club lengths of the nearest dry land that is no nearer the hole than your original lie. No penalty.

HITTING FROM HILLSIDES

Most people practice shots from level lies at the driving range and then wonder why they can't make solid contact from hilly lies on the course. To me this makes about as much sense as preparing for a Channel swim in a bathtub. So take some time to master sidehill lies when you practice. Just one hour of such practice will give you enough skill and confidence on these shots to save you hundreds of strokes over the next few years of play.

The big challenge on hillside shots is keeping your balance so that you can solidly contact the ball, instead of the air above it or the hill beneath it. No matter what type of lie you might have—uphill, downhill, sidehill—you'll need to find a way to keep from falling down the slope as you swing.

I solve this balance problem by addressing the ball with my weight set primarily on my "high" foot, or on the "high sides" of my feet. You'll see what I mean as I describe each of the four varieties of hillside lies.

My least favorite lie is the downhiller, largely because the hill slopes downward in the same direction I'm swinging. Both the force

PLAYING HILLSIDE LIES

DOWNHILL LIES

On downhill lies I play the ball farther back in my stance so that I'll catch it, cleanly, instead of the hill behind it. I flex my right knee and set my weight largely on my right foot so I won't fall to the left and down the hill as I swing. Flexing my right knee also makes my chest level, as I want it. In fact, I imagine a carpenter's level running across it to help me make sure it's set horizontally. I align myself and aim slightly more to the left than I normally would to compensate for the slice that usually results from this lie.

UPHILL LIES

Again I set my chest horizontally, imagining that I've got a carpenter's level running across it. To do this I must flex my left knee more than normally, which puts most of my weight on the left foot. I like my weight to the left so that I won't fall back to the right—down the hill—as I swing. I play the ball in its normal spot—about opposite my left heel—but I align and aim less to the left than normally since these uphillers tend to hook in that direction.

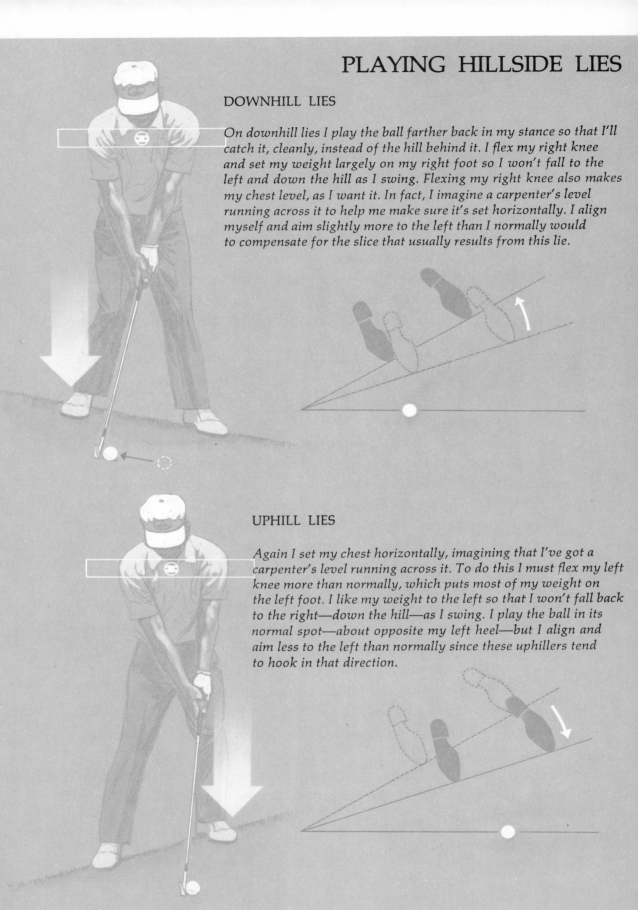

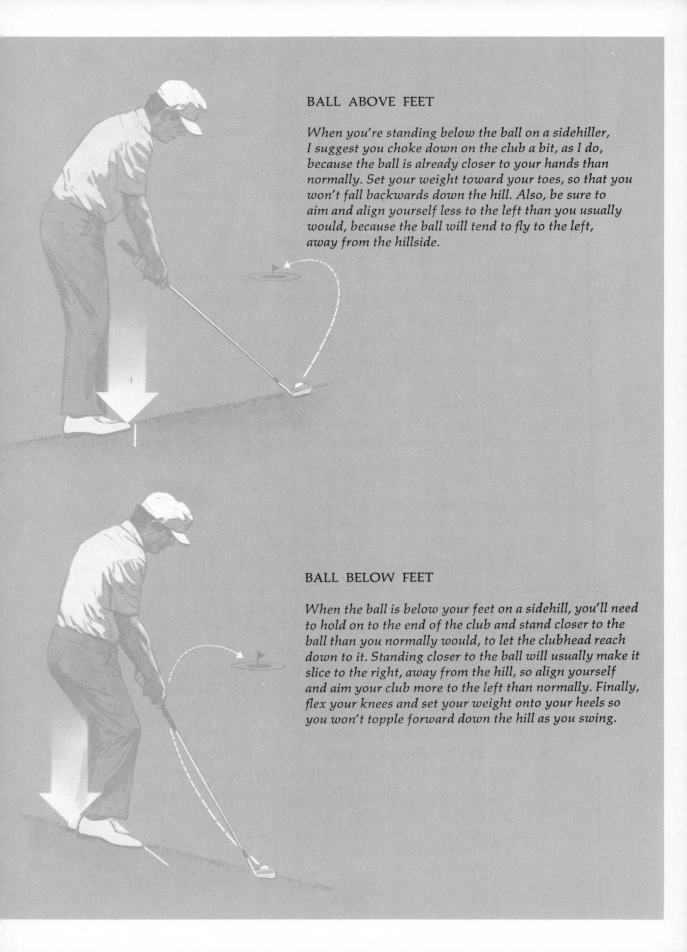

BALL ABOVE FEET

When you're standing below the ball on a sidehiller, I suggest you choke down on the club a bit, as I do, because the ball is already closer to your hands than normally. Set your weight toward your toes, so that you won't fall backwards down the hill. Also, be sure to aim and align yourself less to the left than you usually would, because the ball will tend to fly to the left, away from the hillside.

BALL BELOW FEET

When the ball is below your feet on a sidehill, you'll need to hold on to the end of the club and stand closer to the ball than you normally would, to let the clubhead reach down to it. Standing closer to the ball will usually make it slice to the right, away from the hill, so align yourself and aim your club more to the left than normally. Finally, flex your knees and set your weight onto your heels so you won't topple forward down the hill as you swing.

of my swing and the slope itself then want to throw me down the hill.

On these shots I imagine that I've got a carpenter's level strapped across my chest. If you've never seen one of these tools, it's a piece of board with some glass-enclosed fluid showing on its top side. In the fluid is a bubble, and when the bubble floats to a certain spot, you know the board itself is horizontal.

I try to set my shoulders and chest level so that this imaginary bubble would prove my upper body to be horizontal instead of tilted downward to my left with the slope of the hill. To set myself level, I must really flex my right leg, which is on the higher part of the hill, and the steeper the hill, the more I must bend this leg at the knee. This flexing puts my weight onto my "high" foot so I won't tend to fall down the hill as I swing.

On this shot, I also play the ball farther back in my stance than normal—more opposite my right foot than my left. The steeper the hill, the farther back I play the ball. This rearward positioning lets me contact the ball solidly, instead of digging into the hill behind it or sweeping over the top of it.

I set up to every downhill shot with my feet and shoulders aligned, and my clubface aimed, even more to the left of target than normal. I do this because the tendency on downhill lies is to slice the ball to the right. Aligning and aiming to the left makes the slice I know is coming at least finish in play. Also, because playing the ball back in your stance does reduce the height of the shot, you may need to use a club with more loft than normal, especially on long shots where you might be tempted to use a 3 or 4 wood.

The adjustments I make on uphill lies are the exact opposite of those I make for downhillers, except that I like to play the ball opposite my left heel, which is about where I'd normally play it on a level lie. Instead of overflexing my right leg, I overflex my left leg to make my chest and shoulders level. This again puts most of my weight on my high foot to keep me from falling down the hill as I swing.

Instead of aiming and aligning farther than normal to the left, to avoid slicing, I aim and align more to the right, to offset the normal hooking you get on the uphiller. I usually choose a less lofted club than normal, because the uphill shot tends to fly higher than you'd expect.

On sidehill lies the first thing you must do is set your weight *toward* the hill, to avoid falling down it as you swing. Thus, if the ball is above your feet, you'll set your weight toward your toes to avoid falling back on your heels, and if the ball is below your feet, you'll set back on your heels (again, the high part of your feet) to keep from falling on your face.

Next, you should adjust for the distance the ball is from your hands. If the ball is above your feet, you'll want to choke down on the club to offset its nearness to your hands. If it's below your feet, you'll need to grip at the end of the shaft and stand closer to the ball, to compensate for its being farther than normal from your hands.

Finally, you'll need to adjust for the fact that on these shots the ball will usually fly *away* from the hillside. It will fly to your left when the ball is above your feet—so aim and align more to the right—and it will fly to the right when it's below your feet—so aim and align more to the left.

My last thought on all hillside lies is to swing easily. The easier swing will further help you to retain balance on the slope, but it may mean you'll need to use more club—less loft—than normal.

THIN LIES

When you find your ball sitting on bare ground, or in a divot mark, or deep in lush fairway grass, your main thought should be to contact it just *before* the end of your downswing, when your clubhead is still moving slightly downward. Any attempt to sweep the ball upward will almost surely make you "skull" or "top" the shot, with your clubhead catching the ball on or above its equator. The ball will then either dribble along the ground or nosedive quickly, endangering any worms in its path.

To catch the ball on your downswing, merely play it slightly farther back than normal in your stance. Try to pinch the ball downward with the clubhead. It will backspin up the clubface during impact and then fly strongly upward, even from a very tight lie. A firm left hand and forearm, pulling the clubhead sharply downward to the ball, will also help you catch it on your downswing instead of on your upswing.

With some practice you'll be surprised how high you can make the ball fly, even from a fairly deep divot mark. If you should find that these shots fly to the right of your target—a normal result of playing the ball back in your stance—merely aim your clubface a few degrees farther to the left as you address the ball, but be sure to avoid the tendency to open it back to the right through impact.

SHOTS FROM ROUGH

To be a good player from rough you need sound judgment, good technique, and solid muscle. I can't give you muscles, but I can explain proper judgment and technique.

Judgment applies when you select your club. Too many people use too little loft from rough. The lie of the ball in the grass may call for an 8-iron loft to make it clear the grass and fly freely, but they'll swing a 6 iron because the green is 6-iron distance away. The 6 iron grabs in the grass, the ball catches in it, and the shot dribbles into the fairway or stays in the cabbage.

What you should remember is that a ball comes out of rough "hot," which means that it carries relatively little backspin and therefore drives forward with maximum roll on landing—that is, if you use enough loft in the first place to get it freely airborne. So choose plenty of loft and you'll be surprised how far such a shot will actually travel.

140

Very few golfers are skilled enough, or strong enough, to hit a 2 or 3 iron, or even a 4 iron, from any rough that's much longer than fairway grass. Most would do far better with a 5 iron or a 5 or 6 wood. The woods are more efficient than long irons from light rough because they pancake the grass without having to chop through it.

When it comes to technique, the idea is to catch the ball as crisply as possible before the clubhead has a chance to slush through a lot of grass behind it. Playing the ball a bit farther back in your stance than normal helps you swing into it on a steep angle, thus avoiding much of this grass. Standing a bit closer to it than normal and choking down on the club slightly also puts your swing on a more upright plane for a sharper angle of descent to the ball.

Beyond that, I advise a firm grip with the left hand to minimize the tendency of the clubhead to turn when it snarls in the grass. In fact, on all shots from deep rough I use the ten-finger grip (Chapter 2) and advise that you try it too. This grip restricts wristiness and thus gives me extra firmness as I swing through the grass.

At times you'll find yourself in deep grass near a green. The problem here is to swing forcefully enough to make the ball clear the rough, but not so forcefully that it won't hold the green. What I do on these shots is open the clubface slightly to the right, to give it enough loft to make the ball clear the grass. Then I swing it forcefully downward, on a steep angle of attack, and into the turf *behind* the ball. The forceful swing gets the fast-moving clubhead through the grass, but the turf behind the ball then slows it down so that the ball doesn't overshoot the target. The ball comes up soft and high because of the decreased clubhead speed and the extra loft that is added by opening the face at address. You'll find this same technique works well from a bare lie near the green, but this shot takes extensive practice. Actually, the shot is practically identical to a basic explosion shot from sand. In fact, it's best to play from the bare lie with the sand wedge, so long as you drive it sharply downward into the ground behind the ball.

BUNKER SHOTS

Back at Tenison Park in Dallas, where I played most of my early golf, we didn't have any sand. So when I came out on tour, bunker play was the worst part of my game. I'd leave about one shot out of five in the trap, but that just made me put my nose to the grindstone. I watched how people like Sam Snead, Gardner Dickinson, Gary Player, and Chi Chi Rodriguez played from sand, and I learned a lot from them. Today I feel there's only one player on tour who can beat me out of sand—Gary Player—and even he can't beat me every day.

The first thing you need to play sand shots well is a good sand wedge, one that has enough "bounce" to handle the type of sand you play most frequently. By "bounce" I mean the degree to which the leading edge of the club's sole is higher than its trailing edge. The more bounce you have—the lower hanging the trailing edge—the less the club will cut into the sand, all things being equal.

If you play in soft, fine-grained sand, which offers little resistance to the clubhead, you'll want more bounce on your sand wedge, because the lower trailing edge acts like a rudder to keep the clubhead from cutting in too deeply. If you play in coarse sand, which resists the clubhead, you'll want less bounce—a lower leading edge—to provide better penetration.

Once you find a wedge with the proper amount of bounce for the type of sand you usually encounter, you'll find you can still control the depth of cut it takes by the way you position the clubface at address. The more you open the clubface to the right at address, the more the trailing edge lowers and the leading edge rises. This, in effect, gives you more bounce, or less penetration into the sand. Conversely, the more you close the clubface, the more the leading edge tilts downward, for less bounce and deeper penetration.

On normal sand shots I play the ball about opposite my left heel and I stand wide open, aligned well to the left of my target. I aim the clubface at the target, or slightly to the right if I want a really shallow cut of sand. I dig my feet into the sand so I can still use my legs despite the loose underfooting.

I swing the club up and down on a very upright plane, making sure that my clubhead cuts into the sand about an inch behind the ball. By making it enter the sand this same distance behind the ball on all normal sand shots, I can control the length of the shot by the length and force of my swing, just as I would on a normal pitch shot from the fairway. I'd rather do it that way than control the shot's length by varying my point of entry into the sand.

When I find my ball is buried in the sand, I play a shot that I've never seen anyone else try. Most golfers play the buried lie by cutting into the sand with the clubhead square or closed to the left, to make sure that its leading edge will dig well downward and under the buried ball. Personally, I don't care for this technique because the ball comes out too low and too hot. I want a softer shot with more backspin that will settle quickly on even a small area of green.

So what I do is play the ball back about in the center of my stance, with most of my weight on my left foot. Then I swing the club practically straight up and down. I almost, you might say, give the back of the ball a downward judo chop with the clubface—just stick the clubhead in the sand with no follow-through. The ball rides up the clubface, taking on tremendous backspin, then flies up the sand in front of it nice and high and floats onto the green like a feather dropping on a pond. However, I suggest you first try this shot in practice to see if you're precise enough to catch the ball itself, instead of the sand behind it.

In wet sand you'll need to apply your basic sand shot, but with a bit more force than normal, because the moist and heavy sand will tend to resist clubhead penetration. In fact, I advise most golfers to use their pitching wedges out of wet sand. Since these clubs carry no bounce—the leading edge of the sole is *lower* than the trailing edge— they will easily slice through wet sand that a sand wedge would merely slap against.

143

7 PLAYING AROUND THE GREENS

IF THERE'S AN ELEMENT of golf that's lost out in the era of modern technology, it's the art of chipping and pitching short shots from around the greens. You missed more greens in the old days because they were built as small as postage stamps. If you couldn't get it up and down in two from off the edge, you might as well trade in your Kroydons. Today, instead of a postage stamp they give you the whole envelope. Missing a green is like missing the Grand Canyon.

Also, in the old days architects like the famed Donald Ross would get out there, with a couple of horses pulling a shovel, and contour all sorts of mounds and valleys around the putting surfaces. ("Let's dump three and a half more scoops right here, Charley, and skim out fourteen inches over there.") The result was a never-ending variety of hillside lies to add further intrigue to the short shots. To-day's tractors grade gentle slopes, but not the bumps and dips. Modern gang mowers would shave the mounds bare anyway—which I guess is the chief reason for the change.

Golf carts have also helped ruin the art of chipping and pitching.

Today a golfer drives his cart wide of the green, parks it fifty feet from his ball, and pulls what he *hopes* will be the right chipping club from his bag. If it turns out to be the wrong selection, he goes with it nevertheless, rather than return to the cart for a different club. He doesn't really care that much about chipping anyway.

All these things have contributed to the extinction of chipping and pitching practice. Today you can drive up to the average country club practice area and see about three dinosaurs for every golfer who's out there working on pitch-and-run shots.

Yet, that same club will be filled with men wondering why they now hit the ball better than ever, yet fail to match the scores they shot as youngsters, when they spent hours at a time chipping to tin cans around the caddie yard.

In his heyday Ben Hogan probably hit more greens than any player in the history of the game. Yet, I'm told, he would practice short shots from *off* the green for hours on end, day after day. Isn't that interesting—and educational!

What Hogan probably realized was that over half the strokes wasted in golf take place within thirty yards of the green. I'd guess he also found out, as I have, that chipping and pitching practice is one of the best ways to develop touch, feel, hand-eye coordination, rhythm, tempo, and all those other sensitivities that you need on your *full* shots.

So start working on your chipping and pitching, and watch your handicap slip lower and lower.

Chip shots and pitch shots are similar in that they both take place fairly close in to the green. They are different animals, however, in at least two major respects—the amount of spin applied to the ball and the height it rises into the air.

The ideal chip is a shot that flies low and carries little or no backspin. It lands a few feet onto the green and then bounces and rolls freely forward to the hole. You can chip with any iron club in the bag, except, of course, the putter.

145

The pitch shot flies high and carries considerable backspin. Properly played, it plops down near the flagstick and pulls up short like a duck landing on water. It's usually played with one of the wedges—pitching or sand—for maximum loft and backspin.

The first rule of pitching or chipping is, whenever possible, to land the ball on the smoother surface of the green instead of the rougher, varying surface of the fairway or the fringe. Landing on the green reduces the risk of bad bounces. There will be times when it's impossible to land on the green and still stop the ball before it runs far past the hole. Then landing the ball short and running it onto the green is your only alternative, even though it's second-best.

The next rule usually applies only on shots from the edge of the green and on out from the green fifteen or twenty yards. This rule is to play the *lowest* possible shot that you can make land safely on the green without running well past the hole. For instance, if you have a situation where you can chip a low 4-iron shot onto the green without its running past the hole, don't try to fly a higher shot with a 5 iron or 6 iron.

The advantage in using the least lofted club possible is that the extra roll it provides reduces the length of swing you'll need to make. And the shorter your stroke, the less chance you have of mis-hitting the ball. A short, crisp 4-iron chipping stroke, made largely with the arms, is a far surer way to run a ball across forty to fifty feet of green than the longer, wristier pitching stroke you'd need to carry the ball the same distance with a wedge.

So try to carry your shots onto the green whenever you can, and do it with the least lofted shot that will stop the ball's roll in time to finish near the hole, at least whenever you're within fifteen or twenty yards of the green.

The one exception to these rules would be the occasion when you can actually putt from off the edge of the green. If you don't have more than three or four feet of fringe to roll the ball through, if the grass is consistently short and sparse, and if the ball sets up in a good lie or rests on flat hardpan, the putt is the safest shot.

As you move farther away from the green, beyond fifteen to twenty yards, you'll find it more and more difficult to control distance with the less lofted clubs. For instance, on a twenty-five-yard shot with, say, a 4 iron, you'll find that even a slight bit of extra steam in your stroke will send the ball rolling well over the green. Conversely, a slightly weak stroke may land it short.

Thus pitching takes over from chipping once you move out from the green a certain distance. What this distance is will vary with the player, depending on whether he's better at pitching with the wedges or chipping with less lofted clubs.

The third rule in chipping or pitching is to plan the shot before you select the club. Shot planning demands that you consider several different factors, the first of which is the lie of the ball in the grass.

Generally speaking, the worse your lie, the more important it is to contact the ball on your downswing rather than at the very bottom of your swing arc. If the ball sits down in heavy grass or rests on relatively bare ground, the worst thing you can do is hit the ground behind it. Therefore you must "trap" the ball with your clubhead on your downswing before it has a chance to dig into the grass or cut into the ground. If the ball sets up nicely on top of the grass, it's easier to sweep it away at the bottom of your swing. I certainly would never advise you to try swinging *up* to the ball on your through swing, no matter how high it sets in the grass.

All this means that the poorer your lie, the more you must play the ball back in your stance—toward your right foot—to make sure your clubhead catches the ball before it encounters the turf. Because playing the ball back in your stance takes loft off your club—you can turn a 7 iron into a 4 iron if you play the ball just three or four inches farther back in your stance—you can see how the ball's lie directly affects club selection.

147

AROUND THE GREEN, PICK THE CLUB THAT FITS THE SHOT

Half the battle on short shots around the green is choosing the right club to fit the type of shot you wish to play. The first rule is always to try to land the ball on the green instead of the rougher fairway grass. Next, whenever possible plan a shot that will run freely forward without going far past the hole. That means using the least-lofted club possible, so that you can make the shortest swing possible. Many factors enter into proper club selection, which we discuss in this chapter. Here, however, I give you an idea of the clubs I'd use in various situations, given a normal lie.

8 IRON

I'd choose an 8 iron for this shot because with it I could carry the ball safely onto the green at a height that would allow it to bounce and roll to the hole, but not too far past.

PITCHING WEDGE

From this far out I can't play a chip shot that would land on the green and stop in time. I need to play a high pitch shot that will land near the hole and stop quickly, so I'd choose a pitching wedge or a sand wedge.

4 IRON

Here I'm near the edge of the green and have a lot of real estate between the edge of it and the hole. I can play a low running shot that will land on the green and roll a long way, so I choose a 4 iron. If I used a more lofted club to hit a higher shot, I'd need to make a longer swing, and that longer swing adds to the risk of mis-hitting the ball.

6 IRON

Here I have less green than when I chose the 4 iron and more than I had with the 8 iron, so I'd use a 6 iron. Again, I just want to land the ball safely on the green and roll it freely toward the hole without going way past it.

PITCHING WEDGE

Normally, if I were this close to the green and had this much green between my ball and the hole, I'd chip with a 7 iron or 8 iron. However, because of the downhill slope I need more height to make the ball land softly and stop in time. So I'd probably chip with my pitching wedge.

PUTTER

Whenever you are just a foot or two off the green in a good lie, with short smooth grass leading up to the putting surface, your safest shot is to putt the ball.

SAND WEDGE

Here I have very little green to work with, so I need a high, soft shot that will really stop quickly. Since I have a good lie, I'll choose my most lofted club, the sand wedge, and play it like a normal shot from the fairway.

Another variable to consider in club selection is the overall length of the shot and the amount of green between your ball and the hole. Generally, the *more* green you have and the shorter the distance *to* the green, the less loft you'll need to make the ball land on the green and stop by the hole. If you're twelve feet off the green with twenty-five feet of green to the hole, you might be able to chip with a 7 iron or 8 iron. But if the numbers are reversed—ball twenty-five feet from the edge with only twelve feet of green—you'd need a higher, softer shot with a pitching or sand wedge.

Other variables to be considered are the slope of the green (uphill or downhill), the dampness or dryness of the grass, the texture of the grass (long and thick or short and sparse), the softness or hardness of its subsoil, and even the time of day (fresh-cut greens play faster at 9 A.M. than they will at 5 P.M., after a day's growth).

Quite frankly, I can't tell you how to choose the right club under all the varying conditions. You can learn that only through practice and experience. What I can tell you is that, although you'll never get it all down perfectly every time, the more you learn and the more you observe conditions, the better chipper and pitcher you'll become.

What I can also do is suggest strongly that you always plan your shot beforehand as best you can. Make a positive decision as to how you expect the ball to fly from the lie at hand, and how it will most likely react on the green on shots with various clubs. Choose the club you think will do the best job of producing the shot you want to play. Then use that club, even if you've got to trot over and pull it off your golf cart. (Or, better yet, to save time, take a number of clubs with you when you leave the cart.)

When it comes to the technique of playing chip and pitch shots, the first rule that applies to both is that you make your clubhead *accelerate through* the ball. Anytime your clubhead decelerates before contact, you run the risk of hitting into the ground behind the ball or catching it thin on your upstroke. This applies to all shots in golf, but especially to the less forceful strokes around the green.

150

To accelerate your clubhead into the ball you must think in terms of swinging *through* it, not *to* it. On the precise short shots it's very easy to become "ball-bound" in your efforts to make solid contact. That can lead to your slowing down or guiding the club. So make a firm, crisp forward stroke with your left hand and arm continuing out toward your target. Think of your ball as something that just happens to be in the way of the clubhead, not something you must strike squarely.

Another cause of deceleration is forgetting about your target. Once your mind switches from thinking about the target, it will go back to thinking about the ball, and that leads to deceleration. So always keep your target in your mind's eye as you make your stroke.

Some golfers like to chip or pitch to a certain spot on the green: they size up the shot and choose a club based on where they want the ball to land, then use that landing spot as the target, rather than the hole itself. I did this myself when I played most of my golf at Tenison Park. Because I knew those greens down to the last blade of grass, I could pick the right spot almost every time. I've found I can't spot-chip like this on the tour, however, because my lack of familiarity with the greens too often makes me pick the wrong landing point. So now I use the hole itself as my target. I'm not saying that spot-chipping is wrong; just that it won't work so well on courses you don't play day in and day out.

The second principle of chipping and pitching is that you must swing *down* to the ball to make it go up. On these short shots many golfers try to "help" the ball up by lifting it or scooping at it. In either case, the club's leading edge catches the side or top of the ball while moving upward and the ball dribbles or skims along the ground.

To avoid this problem you must swing the clubhead *down* to the ball so that it makes contact *before* it cuts into, or brushes, the grass in front of the ball's position. When struck with a downward blow, the ball spins up the clubface and then flies away into the air.

151

HOW I CHIP AND PITCH

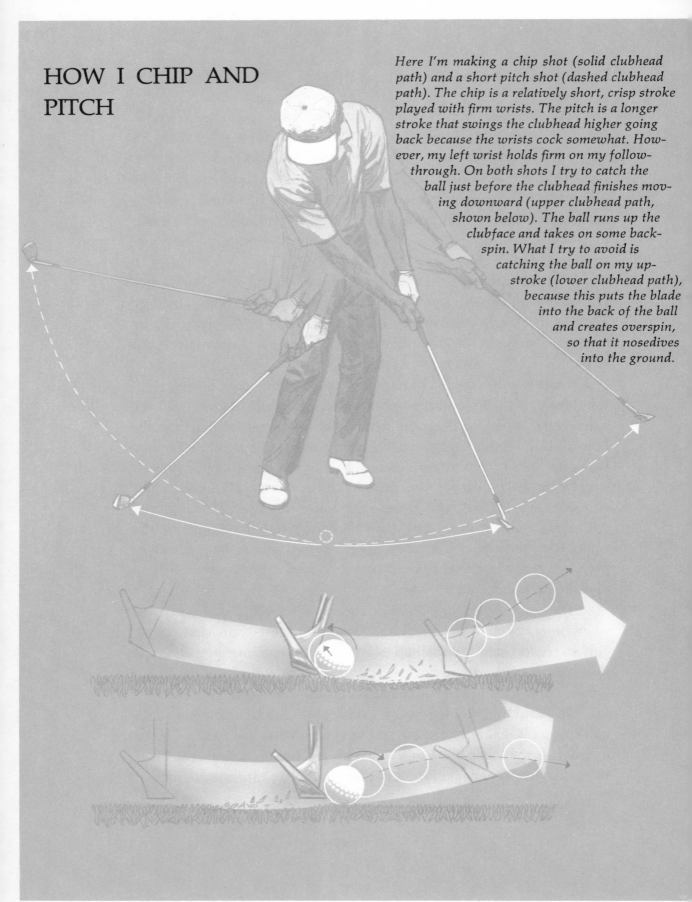

Here I'm making a chip shot (solid clubhead path) and a short pitch shot (dashed clubhead path). The chip is a relatively short, crisp stroke played with firm wrists. The pitch is a longer stroke that swings the clubhead higher going back because the wrists cock somewhat. However, my left wrist holds firm on my follow-through. On both shots I try to catch the ball just before the clubhead finishes moving downward (upper clubhead path, shown below). The ball runs up the clubface and takes on some backspin. What I try to avoid is catching the ball on my upstroke (lower clubhead path), because this puts the blade into the back of the ball and creates overspin, so that it nosedives into the ground.

On chip shots, where you want less backspin and more free forward rolling of the ball, the angle of downward movement should be less steep—just enough to assure meeting the ball before the turf. Thus the ideal chip shot is made largely with the arms, the wrists holding fairly firm. On pitch shots, where some backspin is needed to stop the ball quickly on the green, a steeper angle of attack is desirable. Cocking the wrists during the backswing sets the club high enough for it to swing sufficiently downward to the ball. Even then, however, you need a firm, accelerating left arm, wrist, and hand on the forward swing to drive the clubhead down and through the ball and into the turf beyond. Too much uncocking of the wrists on the downswing can throw the clubhead into the ground behind the ball or flip it upward into its backside.

Thus the chip shot is more of a shallow stroke than the pitch shot, with the arms, rather than the wrists, doing most of the work. Also, since the chip shot is a shorter stroke than the pitch, it requires little or none of the leg movement you'll find helpful on the longer pitch shots.

As to ball position, I like to play my normal pitch and chip shots more or less opposite a spot just inside my left heel. But if I have a tight lie, or if I want to put additional spin on a pitch shot, or if I want to play a low pitch shot into the wind—a "punch shot," in other words—I'll play the ball back in the center of my stance, or even back off my right foot. The farther back I play the ball, the lower the shot I'll make but the more backspin it will carry.

I've mentioned the two most common errors in chipping and pitching—decelerating the clubhead and trying to lift or scoop the ball. A third is setting up to these short shots with the body and feet aligned too far to the left and/or with the hands set too low. Setting up this way can lead to shanking—hitting the ball on the neck of the club instead of the face. What happens is that the right hip gets in the golfer's way during his downswing. This forces his hands, and the clubhead, outside their proper paths. Thus, if you run into the shanks on these shots, simply align yourself less to the left of your flight path and hold your hands a bit higher at address.

One final suggestion: Several of the best chippers actually hold the club using the same grip as they use when putting. I think this makes good sense because in both putting and chipping you want a free arm swing with little or no wrist action. If your putting grip helps keep your wrists "quiet" *on* the greens, I suggest you also try using it on the short shots *to* the greens.

8 SCORING WITH THE PUTTER

I'M GOING TO JUMP into this chapter with the idea that you feel your putting needs help. If you're already a good putter, you should count your blessings and leave well enough alone. Don't change.

If you're putting badly, it's because of one or more of the following: (1) you've got a bad putter, (2) you've got a bad attitude, (3) you've got a bad system for planning putts, or (4) you've got a bad stroke.

You might tell me that you've also got bad luck, and I'm sure you have at times, but luck evens out in the long run. If you'll attend to the other four causes of bad putting I've just mentioned, you'll find yourself getting luckier and luckier.

THE STROKE

I'd like to talk about the stroke first because the way you stroke the ball on the green influences the other problem areas—your attitude, your system for planning putts, and the type of putter you should use.

A good putting stroke is simply one that *consistently* contacts the ball *solidly* while the putterhead is: (1) moving straight down the initial path of the putt, (2) facing down that path, and (3) moving at the right speed. Let's look closely at that sentence because it involves everything I'm going to say about the putting stroke.

I stressed the word "solidly" because, if you can't make solid contact consistently, you'll never be a great putter. Every putter's face has a "sweet spot." That's the spot you should try to lay on the back of the ball during every stroke. This is important because the distance and direction a putt travels is determined largely by where contact is made on the putterface.

Let's say you're on the first green during your Saturday round and you've got a twenty-five-footer for a birdie. You stroke the ball with what you think is the proper amount of force, but it comes up short. Your first reaction will probably be that the greens are slower than you'd thought. A more likely explanation might well be that the greens are normal, and you struck your putt with proper force, but you missed the sweet spot, by perhaps one-quarter to three-eighths of an inch. Even that amount of off-striking could cause your twenty-five-foot putt to come up two or three feet short and a foot or so off the line.

But you don't realize you mis-struck this opening putt, so you go on to the next green and find yourself with another twenty-five-footer. This time you swing with a bit more juice because you suspect the greens are slow. Now you make solid contact. The ball runs over the hole and finishes five feet beyond. The rest of the round you're agonizing over every putt—short on one, long on the next.

To find your putter's sweet spot, merely suspend it in mid-air in front of you by holding the grip end lightly with your thumb and forefinger. Then, with your other forefinger, tap the face of the putter at various spots until you find the spot that makes the putterhead rebound straight back without twisting. That will be the club's sweet spot, and that's where you should try to contact all your putts.

If you contact the sweet spot every time, you'll be on your way to solid putting, but only if you can also strike your putts with the putterhead moving down the initial path of the putt with the face looking in that same direction. If your putterface looks in a different direction than it's moving, you'll put a glancing blow on the ball. It will then spin off line as it starts rolling and often come up short. Of course, even if your putter's looking in the same direction as it's moving, you won't have much success if it's not moving on the right path. You'll get a solid strike, but in the wrong direction.

The surest thing I know about putting is that your putterhead cannot be moving *down* your line at contact if it has started its for-ward movement, back to the ball, from *outside* that line. Once it starts forward from the outside, it must be moving across the line, back to the inside, when it meets the ball. Then the only way to make the putt go on line is to compensate for the cross-line movement to the left by opening the putterface to the right. Which, of course, gives you a glancing blow.

So make sure your putterhead *never* moves outside your line during your stroke. This is a common problem that many golfers don't know they have. I suggest you practice putting some balls that you've set about two inches from the base of a wall at home. Check to see if your putterhead does, in fact, move straight back from the ball on your backstroke—even a little to the inside is O.K., but *never* across the line to the outside so that it bumps the wall.

If you find that your putterhead is moving to the outside, merely continue practice stroking along the wall until you regroove the proper stroke. For a time it will feel as if you're routing the putter back around your right foot, even though you're actually taking it straight back or slightly inside.

I think you'll find it easier to stroke back and through on a straight line, or back slightly to the inside and then straight through,

THREE KEYS TO CONSISTENT PUTTING

Consistent putting starts with striking the ball on the putter's "sweet spot" every time. Missing the sweet spot makes any given putt finish shorter than it normally would. Find your putter's sweet spot by holding it as shown here and tapping the face with your forefinger until you find the spot that makes the club rebound straight back without twisting.

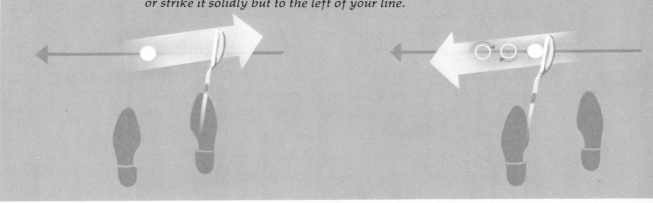

If you swing your putter outside your line going back, you must either apply a glancing blow to the ball that makes it spin sideways, or strike it solidly but to the left of your line.

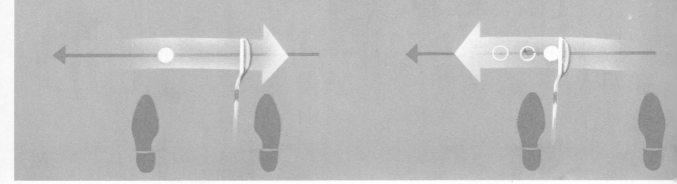

By setting my feet on a line that's parallel to my putting line, I find it easier to swing my putterhead back and forward on the line. This gives me solid contact with no sidespin.

I feel that a firm-wristed stroke, with my arms swinging like a pendulum, is more consistent than one that relies largely on wristiness. I try to swing the grip end of my putter back and forward with the putterhead so that my arms create the stroke. I try to accelerate my left hand and arm forward on all strokes, so that my right hand doesn't take over and flip the putterhead upward or off line.

if you start from a square stance. Set your feet so that a line across your toes would parallel the initial path of your putt. I know I've told you to align to the left on your shots *to* the green, but aligning with an open stance on putts can make you swing the putter back outside the line. Setting up in a closed stance—feet aligned to the right—might help you take it back straight or slightly inside the line, but it might also make it difficult for you to accelerate the putterhead through the ball on the forward stroke.

If swinging on the proper path and striking the ball on the sweet spot are important elements of good putting, it's also important to make sure that you always *accelerate* your putter forward *through* the ball. I can't think of a shot in golf where you shouldn't at least try to accelerate, but acceleration is most important on putts, especially on those putts where it would seem least necessary—the short ones.

Acceleration through the ball keeps your putterhead moving down the line, looking in that direction, and continuing forward low to the ground. Deceleration may cause scuffing, pulling to the left, opening the face to the right, or swinging upward to the ball so that you top it slightly.

Deceleration often results from a backstroke that's too long, in that you sense you're going to roll the ball too far past the hole, then decelerate on the forward stroke to compensate.

A good practice technique that I sometimes use is to purposely make a backstroke that's too short for the length of the putt. I may swing the putterhead back only two or three inches on a thirty-five foot putt. I know that may sound ridiculous, but it does breed the feeling for acceleration that you need in the stroke. If I do this a few times in practice, I'll start to accelerate automatically, without even thinking about the length of my stroke.

Another reason people decelerate in putting is that they play the ball so far forward in the stance that the left arm slows down or stops before the putterhead ever reaches the ball. Then all they can do is

160

flip the clubhead forward with the right hand, causing the left wrist to break down—to cup inward—which is a sure way to misalign the face and catch the ball on the upstroke.

Thus I suggest you play the ball no farther forward than off the inside of your left heel on all normal putts, so that you can keep that left arm charging forward all the way through contact with the ball. Never let it decelerate in such a way that your right hand must take over.

If you have trouble on those three- and four-footers—and who doesn't?—try playing the ball even farther back in your stance, at about equal distance between your feet. This is a tip that Jack Burke, Jr., once gave me and it really works. By playing the ball farther back in your stance, you actually position your left foot closer to the hole than normal. This makes a short putt seem even shorter, which helps a lot with your confidence. Also, if you play the ball back but keep your hands in their normal position, your left hand is in better position to lead the clubhead through the ball, which also encourages acceleration. And with this hand farther forward of the ball, you're less likely to pull the blade to the left or close the clubface before you make contact.

Because I feel acceleration is so important, I prefer arm putting to wrist putting. I think that Bob Charles is the best putter in the world, and he swings his putter entirely with his arms. If you swing your arms freely the way he does, then you're more likely to keep your left arm going forward, even after you've made contact. This keeps the right hand from taking over and flipping the putterhead at the ball. You never see a good arm putter's left wrist break down and cup inward. The arm putter just swings the club like a pendulum and the putterhead seldom leaves the line of the putt. It also stays square to the line a lot better than it will if you start flipping the wrists.

If you want to try arm putting, make sure you set your hands high at address. The lower you set them, the more wristily you'll putt,

161

and thus the more you'll swing your putterhead back and through on a curved arc instead of on a straight line. Of course, the more your putterhead's path is curved, the less your chances that it will be moving down the line and looking straight ahead at contact.

To set your hands high—to "freeze" your wrists, as we'd say on tour—I suggest you hold the putter so that the grip runs up the channel formed *between* the heel pad and the thumb pad of your left hand. On a normal full shot, where you need a certain amount of wrist movement, you'll want to set the shaft under the heel pad, but not on putts, where wrist action can cause problems.

Once you've got your hands set high and the ball opposite the inside of your left heel, then make sure your hands do not trail your putterhead, either at address or during your stroke. The left hand should *always* lead the putterhead back to the ball, and it will if you keep accelerating your left arm forward. I personally prefer to make a slight forward press with my hands just before I start my stroke. I slide them an inch or so to the left just before my takeaway. This breaks tension and also programs my left hand and arm to take the leading role during my forward stroke.

If you plan to become an arm putter, you should make sure that the grip end of the putter swings back and forward during your stroke. This end won't swing quite so far as the putterhead itself, but unless it moves some—I'd say at least half the distance the putterhead moves—you'll find your wrists getting into the act.

I also think you'll find it helpful in developing a free arm stroke if you'll spend some time practicing putts on which you do not sole the putterhead at address. Just let it hang a fraction of an inch off the ground. You'll find this not only gives you a feel for swinging your arms but also builds a nice sense of rhythm into your stroke. I just wish I could make myself take this practice technique onto the golf course; I know I'd putt better if I could. The problem is that sometimes when I'm under pressure I need to sole the putterhead to make it stop shaking.

SUMMARY OF THE PUTTING STROKE

—Find your putter's sweet spot and use it.

—Address the ball from a square stance with your left hand ahead of the ball and both hands high. (Set the clubshaft between the heel and thumb pad of the left hand.)

—Play the ball opposite the inside of the heel of the left foot.

—Swing the putterhead straight back on line or, on long putts, straight back and then gradually to the inside.

—Accelerate your left arm forward through the ball on all putts, so that your left wrist does not cup inward.

FINDING THE RIGHT PUTTER

Some people are driver freaks and some are putter freaks. I hate to admit it, but I'm a putter freak. I've won tournaments where I've used a different putter each of the four days, but I'm not bragging— no, sir! I really envy people like Nicklaus, Casper, and Player, who seldom, if ever, switch putters. Oh, they may occasionally bring a new one out on the putting green for a change of pace, but only because they know that when they go back to their old favorite it will feel 100 percent better.

Arnold Palmer sometimes comes down to the practice green with a half-dozen different putters. In my opinion, all he's doing is carrying a handful of indecisions. A new putter may work wonders for a round or two, but eventually the real cause of the problem—usually a fault in your technique—comes back to haunt you. Then you're torn between which putter to use the next day.

What I'm saying is that if you find a putter that works for you over the long haul, treasure it like you would a good wife. Don't go

163

out playing around, looking for something better. Just keep plugging away with your old friend, even when the going gets tough, and in the end the two of you will enjoy a wonderful relationship.

Choosing the right putter is a highly personal matter, like finding the right bride. There are a million to choose from, but the challenge is to find one that serves your needs.

For instance, do you play most of your golf on slow greens? If so, you'd probably want a putter with a relatively heavy head.

Do you like to set your hands high at address? If so, you'll want a fairly upright putter. Then you'll be able to hold your hands high without setting the putterhead on its toe when you address the ball.

Do you like to set your hands slightly ahead of the ball at address, or do you like to make a little forward press? In either case, you'll probably need a putter with a bit more loft than normal— otherwise its face might be looking downward by the time it returns to the ball.

Do you prefer a stiff-shafted putter or one that flexes slightly? Do you prefer a mallet or blade? Center-shafted or heel-shafted? Round grip or paddle grip? Long or short?

Selecting the right putter won't be as big a chore as perhaps I've led you to believe, but it is important that you make the best possible choice. Any good club professional will no doubt be happy to advise you according to your personal needs, and I'm sure he will let you try out several on the practice green before you make a final decision.

PLANNING YOUR PUTTS

When it come to planning putts, there is no substitute for experience and awareness. It takes time to develop both to a high degree, but you might as well start moving in the right direction now.

Apart from playing a lot of golf, the best way to build experience is to practice seriously on a green that has some slope to it. When you practice, don't just throw down four or five balls and try to knock them into the hole. On the course you don't get four or five chances, so why practice as if you do? To really develop some sense of distance and direction, and to really learn how to judge slopes and grain and speed, it makes much more sense to me to practice with just one ball. With just one try you might not make as many putts, but you'll sure learn a lot from your misses. You'll build a real backlog of experience, and you'll force yourself into becoming more and more aware of the various factors that might influence how a ball reacts on a given putt.

I think any system for planning putts has to start and *end* with the target. Too many golfers carefully plan how they want the ball to get to the hole and then forget about the hole completely. They start thinking about their stroke, or their putterhead, or the ball, or the girl in the pro shop—anything but their goal, which is the *hole*. If you've practiced carefully and thoroughly, all you should need to think about, once you've set up over the ball and aimed, is your target and how your stroke should feel to make the ball go to it. You'll be amazed how well your muscles and nerves will react if you'll simply give them a specific target to shoot for, instead of telling them what specifically to do.

Now that I've talked about target, I've got to tell you that there are times when I don't really try to actually hole the putt, when my target isn't specifically the hole. If I've got a slick green and a ten-foot putt that's going to break eight feet sideways, what I'll be thinking about is where I want the ball to finish to leave me a dead-safe second putt. If it goes in, fine, but my main concern is simply getting close. On these occasions, I've still got the hole in my mind's eye as I putt, but I'm not exactly charging the cup to put the ball in there. Then golf putting becomes a bit like billiards; I'm thinking about my next shot while I'm planning the one at hand.

One thing that many good putters do is separate their thinking into two specific parts. First, they think direction, then distance or speed. Once they've picked the line and aimed the putterface, they

165

switch off "direction" and concentrate on getting just the right feel for distance. I'm sure Jack Nicklaus is going through this process as he stands so long over each putt. And, if I could putt as well as Jack does, I wouldn't mind standing over the ball until the cows come home.

Actually I'm a quick putter. I don't believe in taking a lot of practice strokes and then standing over the ball until my muscles and my brain have a chance to tense up. The more pressure I've got on me for a given putt, the sooner I want to pull the trigger. In the 1971 British Open at Royal Birkdale, I needed a three- or four-footer on the 72nd hole to win. I knocked that one in so fast that it hit the bottom of the cup while the television announcer was still talking about how the ball would break.

In reading greens, I like to get an overall impression before I settle on a specific line. That's why you'll see me wandering all around the place, looking at the putt from the sides as well as from behind the ball. If you look at any breaking putt from both sides, you're sure to see which way it breaks, and more or less how much, merely by comparing the two views you get of the slope. You'll also get a better impression of the distance of the putt, and any uphill or downhill roll on its path, than you would if you merely looked down the line from behind the ball. But don't spend all day sizing up a putt. You can usually look at yours from both sides while others are walking onto the green and fixing the marks their shots have made on landing.

Reading greens isn't only a matter of reading slope; you've also got to consider the length and texture of the grass. If you're playing during the growing season, you'll find a tremendous difference in the speed of your putts if the grass has seen a lot of daylight since it was mowed.

Types of grasses also determine how putts will roll. Bermuda grass, with its thick blades, will putt slower than bent grass. Putts won't break as much because of slope on Bermuda as they will on the slicker bent grasses. But any grain—the direction the grass lies—will have more effect on Bermuda grass than on bent grass.

I've found that grain on Bermuda-grass greens, such as you find in Florida and other southern areas, invariably runs toward the setting sun—to the west—so the ball pulls in that direction. Thus cross-grain putts running north to south or south to north will dribble off to the west. Putts running east to west will roll considerably farther than those that are fighting the grain from west to east.

On a bent-grass green, the grain will usually run in the direction in which any water on its surface would drain. Thus you can figure that any grain on these greens will run down the slope. This makes downhill putts especially slick, and it makes sidehillers break more than you'd normally expect.

In reading the grain and slope of greens, it's important to pay special attention to the area around the hole itself. All things being equal, this portion of the green will take more break than any other because it's been trampled down to a firmer, slicker surface by golfers' feet. Your putt will also be more susceptible to sidehill slope or any cross-grain texture near the hole, because that's where your ball will be rolling its slowest.

My final point about planning putts is to suggest that you always *commit* yourself to a specific line before you set up to the ball. Any second-guessing thereafter will only lower your confidence and increase tension. If doubt strikes while you're over the ball, back away and settle the matter in your mind before proceeding.

BUILDING CONFIDENCE

The best way to build confidence is to succeed. The more you succeed, the more confident you get, and the more confident you get, the more you succeed. All you'll need to do to get this cycle going is to follow the points I've made in this chapter. First, find a putter that you feel at home with. Next, practice. It's as simple as that. Practice the things I've talked about in the section on developing a proper stroke. Practice to build up a background of experience and an awareness for reading greens. Then, armed with a good putter, a solid stroke, and a sound system, you'll hole putts on the course more and more frequently. That success will give you the confidence you'll need to produce even greater success.

9 FINDING CLUBS
THAT FIT YOUR SWING

I DON'T THINK any golf instruction book would be complete without a chapter on clubs. There's no getting around it: the clubs you swing have a lot to do with *how* you swing, for good or for bad. It would be silly to spend dozens of hours trying to improve your swing and then go out and mis-hit a shot because your equipment was faulty. If your clubs don't fit you when your swing is good, then sooner or later you're going to start swinging bad to make yourself adjust to your clubs. Obviously it should be the other way around.

After reading this book and going to all the trouble of improving your technique, the smart move might be to check with your professional to make sure that your sticks suit your new swing. You might find, for instance, that with your new swing you can handle stiffer-shafted clubs than you've been using. If you didn't get the stiffer shafts, you'd probably lose a lot of the accuracy that you deserve with your improved technique.

It's my opinion that millions of golfers are playing with one or more ill-fitting clubs in their bags. If you hit fairly good shots with

169

every club except, say, your 4 iron, then maybe that club doesn't match the rest of your set. Or, if you hit one club better than all the others, perhaps the others should more closely match the club you hit well.

Obviously I can't tell every individual exactly what club specifications he or she should be using, but I can give you a few guidelines and some opinions to help you find a set of clubs that better meets your own personal needs. I honestly believe that there is a particular set of club specifications that is right for you. It may take some time and effort—and expense—on your part to find the right combination, but it's worth it in the long run if you're serious about golf. Why play with a set of clubs that forces you to make a dozen different swings—one for each club? Why not find a set where the same swing works for all?

Just to give you an idea about how much stock I personally put in finding the right clubs, whenever I come across a club that works particularly well, I tear it apart to find out what it's all about. I'll take the head off and weigh it, for instance. I'll test the shaft flex and measure the grip size. I'll check its overall length and weight, and measure its deadweight and swingweight. I'll certainly check its "lie"— the angle formed between the head and the shaft.

Once I've got all this data about the club, I'll log it into a book I keep back in El Paso. I've probably got five or six sets of clubs, and I know everything about every individual club. I could lose all my clubs tomorrow and in no time get myself a set that would match, to the nth degree, the best of what I had.

I know most of you won't want to take all these pains, but I just want you to know how much importance I personally put on having the right clubs for my game. This knowledge I've accumulated not only provides me with better-fitting clubs but also gives me a great boost of confidence in them.

I'll tell you more about the clubs I use as I discuss the various factors you should consider when you buy your own set. First, however, let me just mention one example of how personalized you can get about fitting clubs to your specific needs. This example deals with my wedges.

Two things I want to be able to do with my wedges are, first, hit low shots that won't flutter around in the wind and, second, make them stop quickly, even though they're flying low. Well, I've found that the normal pitching wedge doesn't give me enough backspin because the face isn't quite deep enough from top to bottom. When the ball runs up the face during impact, there isn't enough space and enough grooves to impart the degree of backspin I need to make the ball grab quickly upon landing.

So I've taken sand wedges, which have a deeper face and more grooves, and modified them into pitching wedges. I've bent the heads downward a bit until I've taken about five degrees of loft off the face. This decreased loft makes my shots fly as low or lower than they would with a pitching wedge, even though the sand wedge in its original form carries more loft. I also take a bit of weight out of the head so that the club weighs about the same as a normal pitching wedge.

I've learned the hard way, however, that you do need to be careful when you start using off-beat equipment. I remember a wedge I had back in 1971 that suited me particularly well. Before the British Open that year I asked the officials there to check it to make sure it was legal. They kept it a day and then returned it to me, saying it was O.K. I went on the win the tournament, holing out four times from off the green.

At Augusta the next spring, just before the Masters, Joe Dey, who was then director of the Tournament Players Division of the P.G.A., came up to me and asked if he might take a look at the wedge. Joe had it examined closely by some experts, and they found that the scoring on the face, though it looked grooved to the naked eye, was

HOW YOUR CLUB'S LIE AFFECTS YOUR SHOTS

FLAT   STANDARD   UPRIGHT

A big factor in how you hit your shots is the "lie" of each club in your set. The lie is the angle formed by the shaft and the clubhead as shown above. Manufacturers make clubs of standard lie, as well as those that are flat and upright to varying degrees. It's wise to have a professional fit you with clubs that have the correct lie for your build, posture, and swing. The problems that occur when your clubs' lies do not fit your needs are shown in the drawings on the right.

IF YOUR LIE IS TOO FLAT...

...you will either set your hands too low (dashed line shows proper angling of the shaft), with the clubhead soled flat on the ground, or (see next page)...

IF YOUR LIE IS TOO UPRIGHT...

...you will either set your hands too high (dashed line shows proper angling of the shaft), with the clubhead soled flat on the ground, or (see next page)...

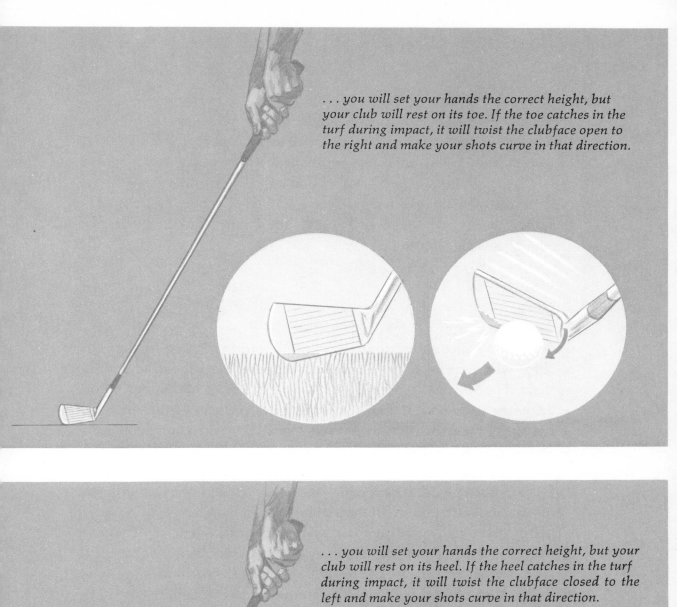

. . . you will set your hands the correct height, but your club will rest on its toe. If the toe catches in the turf during impact, it will twist the clubface open to the right and make your shots curve in that direction.

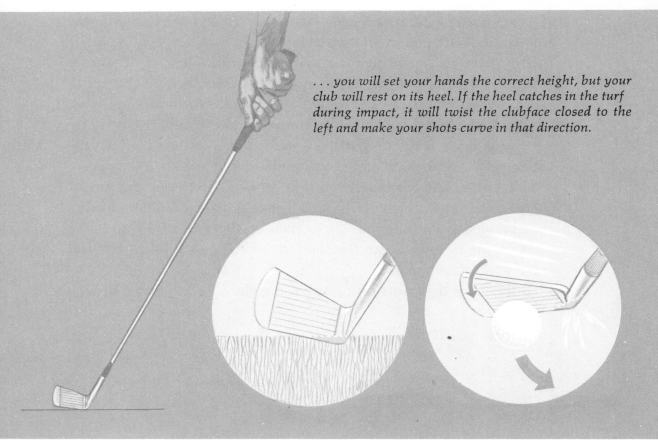

. . . you will set your hands the correct height, but your club will rest on its heel. If the heel catches in the turf during impact, it will twist the clubface closed to the left and make your shots curve in that direction.

actually a series of punched-out indentations. Now, according to the rule on punched scoring, only up to 18 percent of the face may be so scored. They found that my scoring covered 20 percent of the face.

To make a long story short, I had to get rid of the wedge. I gave it to my then British manager, who raffled it off in England. The money went to the Cancer Society, but I never did find out who bought my illegal wedge.

LIE

Perhaps the most important aspect of club fitting is finding the right "lie," which, as I said, is the angle formed between the head and the shaft. The way this works is that, if you've got a club with a proper lie, when you sole it flat on the ground the grip end of the shaft will come up to just the right height for your hands when you adopt your correct address posture.

If your clubs have a lie that's too flat—if there's too little angle formed between the underside of the shaft and the ground (see illustration)—then one of two things must happen. You're either going to set your hands too low and make bad swings, or, if you set them the right height but rest the club on its toe, then you'll tend to slice your shots, because the toe will stub into the turf and slow down during impact so that the whole face twists to the right.

If your lie is too upright—too much angle formed between the underside of the shaft and the ground—the opposite will happen. You'll either set your hands too high, or you'll set them the proper height but rest the club on its heel. The high hands again will cause bad swings, and setting the club on its heel will cause it to grab in the turf during impact so that the clubface swings closed to the left and your shots tend to hook.

I believe that most people are using clubs with lies that are too flat. That's one reason why so many golfers slice their shots. If you've got one or two clubs in your set that you generally hook or slice with, I suggest you ask your pro to check out their lie, because that might be the cause of the problem.

Nine out of ten expert golfers would tell you that the shorter-shafted clubs in any given set should be more upright than the longer-shafted clubs. This would be true to an extent, because we must stand closer to the ball with the shorter shafts. However, I feel that manufacturers are making the short irons *too* upright and the longer irons *too* flat. In my own set, for instance, I've got a "standard" lie on my 4 iron and 5 iron. However, the lie on my 3 iron is one-half degree more upright than standard, and the lie on my 2 iron is one degree more upright. When I work up from the 5 iron in the other direction, into the more lofted clubs, I reverse the process: each higher-numbered club is progressively one-half degree *flatter* than standard. Since my 5 iron is standard lie, my 6 iron is one-half degree flatter than standard, my 7 iron one degree flatter, and so on up to my 9 iron and wedges, which are two degrees flatter than normal.

There's a good reason for varying my lies in this manner. It has to do with the degree to which I accelerate my hips through the hitting area. I'll accelerate them faster on a 2-iron shot, say, than I would on a 5-iron shot. Similarly, I'll accelerate more on the 5-iron shot than on an 8-iron shot, which, in turn, I'll accelerate more than I would on a wedge shot.

The more I accelerate my hips, the greater the chances are that I'll shift too far ahead of the clubhead and thus make contact with the clubface open. The slower I accelerate my hips, the greater the chance that my arms and hands will take over and close the face. So my normal tendency would be to slice my long irons to the right and hook my short irons to the left. I'd say that the vast majority of golfers follow this same pattern.

Therefore, I use the more upright lies—which tend to promote hooking—on my longer clubs to offset the normal tendency to slice with these clubs. Since flatter lies promote slicing, by making my lies flatter on my shorter irons I offset the tendency to hook with these clubs.

I think that club manufacturers could do a great service for golfers if they'd make their longer irons a bit more upright, and the shorter irons a little flatter, than they now make them. In the meantime, however, if you happen to be slicing your long irons and pulling or hooking your short irons, I suggest you ask your pro to make one of the longer-shafted clubs a degree or two more upright, and one of the shorter clubs a degree or two flatter. If these changes make your shots with these two clubs fly straighter, then you might want to modify your whole set.

Along these same lines, it's my personal opinion that Jack Nicklaus, as great as he is, could be a much better wedge player if his wedge wasn't so darned upright. Then he'd be less likely to pull these shots to the left when he doesn't make a full swing with full acceleration, or he'd have less need to compensate in his swing to avoid pulling. You're welcome, Jack.

CLUB LENGTH

Despite what many golfers seem to think, the factor that primarily determines the length of clubs you should use is *not* your height. A more important factor than height is the distance from your fingertips to the ground when you let your arms hang naturally. Another factor that's important is the size of the swing arc you make with your arms and club.

I happen to be a fairly short man at five feet seven, so you might think I'd need clubs that are shorter than standard. Not so! Since my arms are also short—twenty-nine-inch sleeve length—my fingertips are the same *distance from the ground* as those of some men who are almost a foot taller. For that reason, I need shafts of at least standard length in order to avoid crowding the ball.

If anything, I could be using shafts that are *longer* than standard (as does Gary Player, another short man). Generally speaking, I feel that it's the *short* man who needs the longer shafts, not your average tall man. I say this because anyone with short arms (which is most often the case with short people) needs more club length in order to make a big enough swing arc to generate sufficient clubhead speed. The tall man, who generally has fairly long arms anyway, doesn't have so much of a problem making a big arc—his problem is controlling the big arc he's already got. So the tall man who goes to longer shafts too often complicates his swing unnecessarily by increasing the size of his arc.

I'm not saying that some tall men don't need longer clubs, but I certainly wouldn't like to see most of them go to shafts that are any more than one-half inch longer than standard. The exception would be the tall man with very short arms.

However, a short man who has unusually long arms might well consider using clubs that are slightly shorter than standard. With his long arms he might not need a big swing arc anyway, and standard clubs might make him stand too far from the ball, which would make him swing on too flat a plane.

Touring pro Rod Curl is an example of a short man (five feet five) with exceptionally long arms (thirty-five-inch sleeve). Rod can scratch his knees without bending over. Obviously he needs shorter clubs than standard, which is what he does use. Even with shorter clubs, however, he still must stand so far from the ball that he also needs, and uses, clubs with lies that are exceptionally flat.

I hate to generalize about club length because everyone has a different type of swing to some extent, but my rule of thumb would be to suggest that you use standard-length clubs unless you are a short man with short arms or a tall man with relatively short arms. Then you might need longer shafts, but, even then, you should check with your pro before going to any clubs that are more than one-half inch longer than standard or, perhaps, one inch longer in the case of the driver. I wouldn't consider shorter clubs unless you happen to have unusually long arms, which is often the case with women. Women in general, I find, tend to do better with clubs that are shorter and lighter than standard, but this also has to be a generalization.

One more consideration involving shaft length is the tempo or pace of your swing. Longer-shafted clubs demand a slower-paced swing. It's been my experience that a golfer with an unusually fast swing who goes to longer shafts has trouble at first making the necessary adjustment to slow his pace. However, in time and with practice the longer shafts will force such a player into making a slower swing, which is definitely to his or her benefit.

SHAFT FLEX

Golf club shafts come in various degrees of flex or tendency to bend. Finding shafts that will bend just the right amount for your particular swing is certainly an important aspect of club selection.

If, for instance, you get shafts that are too stiff for your swing, you'll lose the tiny bit of additional distance you'd get with the softer shafts, which could give you an extra forward kick into the ball on a well-timed swing. Because stiff shafts are made from thicker metal, they also add a little bit more to the club's overall weight, which might slow down your swing speed. More important, shafts that are too stiff reduce one's feel for the clubhead, which can make timing the swing more difficult.

These are not major drawbacks, however, when compared to the loss of accuracy and distance you might suffer from using shafts that are too flexible. If your shafts are too soft, you'll need near-perfect timing to deliver the clubhead squarely to the ball. The stronger player thus equipped might need to rein in his natural power to keep the clubhead from trailing too far behind his hands into impact. That, in fact, was why Chi Chi Rodriguez was hitting his shots too low and without much accuracy until I suggested he use stiffer shafts that wouldn't flex so much during his downswing.

Generally speaking, the stronger you are and the faster you swing and the better player you are, the stiffer the shafts you should use. Weaker people—most women, juniors, and some seniors, for instance—would get better feel and more clubhead speed with the lighter, softer shafts.

I think the new graphite shafts are terrific for most golfers' driving club—especially women's—because they reduce the overall weight of the club by as much as two ounces, which allows for faster swinging. They do tend to flex more than metal, but they "recover" from the bending very quickly. That means you get little or no loss of accuracy—and probably more distance—if you can find the right combination of shaft flex and clubhead weight for your particular needs.

On the other hand, I do not feel that graphite is all that good in iron clubs, with which you'll normally be contacting the ground and thus flexing the shaft too much during impact.

Various manufacturers use different ways to designate shaft flex, and your pro can explain what they all mean when you select your next set of clubs. I personally prefer the Dynamic S-type shaft, which is a bit stiffer than normal, but not so stiff as an X shaft.

I also want each of my shafts to have a slightly different flex, because I want more stiffness in my shorter clubs than in my longer clubs. Therefore I cut each shaft so that there is a different amount of space between the bottom of the shaft and the first "step," or increase in diameter, from the bottom. For instance, I want a ten and one-half inch space below the first step on my 9 iron, ten and three-quarter inches on my 8 iron, and I increase the space a little more than one quarter of an inch on each of the progressively longer irons. Many manufacturers provide this gradation only on

179

every *other* club, so that, for instance, the 8 iron and 9 iron are identically spaced, as are the 6 iron and 7 iron, and so on. It may seem a small matter, but it shows you how much I want all my clubs to swing like all the others.

GRIP SIZE

I find that the diameter of the grips I use has a tremendous influence on my shots. There are two schools of thought about the size of grips. One school holds that the thinner the grip, the more your wrists come into play, and that thinner grips therefore increase distance and the ability to hook the ball, but lessen accuracy. I've found just the opposite to be true. I'm not saying that thinner grips will cause slicing and thicker grips hooking for everyone, but that's the way it's worked for me.

Once I was playing in Memphis and took my clubs into Bert Dargie's shop there for a new set of grips. I'd been having trouble getting the nice little left-to-right fade I like to play on most of my normal shots. Bert put on some grips that came out to be slightly thinner than I'd been using. My old fade reappeared as soon as I started using those thinner grips.

I asked Bob Toski, the famous teacher of golf, about this at the time. Bob didn't see anything unusual about my fading with the thinner grips. He said that thinner grips tend to make you cut the ball a bit more from left to right. This also held true in 1975 when Tom Weiskopf came up to me at the Ryder Cup Matches, just after he'd missed winning the World Open. He said, "Lee, if I could drive that ball like you do, I'd win six or seven tournaments a year. Everything I hit seems to finish out to the right."

When I hit some shots with Tom's driver, I discovered that the area where the right hand goes on the grip was too thin. I took Tom's club into Arnold Palmer's shop and built up the right-hand grip

180

slightly. Then every day during the matches I'd ask Tom how he'd driven the ball. "Fantastic," he'd say, "absolutely fantastic." He killed them with that thicker grip.

Grip size, like most of the other factors I've discussed, is something you should work out with the pro who's selling you the clubs. He can get you grips that not only fit your particular hands but also will help you hit the shape of shots that you want to hit.

DEPTH OF FACE

On wood clubs especially, the depth of the face—from top to bottom —has a lot to do with how high or low you'll be able to hit your shots. Clubs with shallow faces have most of their mass at a lower point than do clubs with deep faces. The lower the mass, the more force you'll apply to the underside of the ball. Therefore, the shallower the face, the higher you'll hit your shots.

Since most golfers need more height on their shots, I don't recommend deep-faced woods to anyone except the very strong male golfer who gets plenty of height and carry on his shots anyway. Women golfers, especially, need shallow-faced clubs to get the height that they miss out on from not being able to generate a whole lot of clubhead speed. In fact, most women also need more *loft* on their wood clubs, especially the drivers. I think most women, and many men, would be better off driving with a 1½ wood—a club with, say, a 12- or 13-degree loft—instead of a normal driver.

WEIGHT

The trend today seems to be toward lighter clubs, just as it's been toward lighter bats in baseball. The lighter shafts, such as graphite, have helped this trend by giving us clubs that are lighter overall while still being slightly heavier in the clubhead itself.

Obviously, you can swing a lighter club faster than a heavy club, and therefore generate more clubhead speed. But if you get a club that's *too* light, you'll swing it too fast and, I've found, start hooking the ball. The ideal club for you is one that is light enough to swing at the maximum speed you can control but still has enough weight in the head to apply enough mass to the ball to move it a fair distance.

Your pro will help you find the right combination of overall weight and clubhead weight to give you your maximum distance consistently. He'll deal with something called "swingweight," which is a measurement of the weights of the various components of the club—grip, shaft, and head—in relation to each other. Generally speaking, a club with a heavier head and a lighter shaft will run higher on the swingweight scale. A club with a swingweight of C-9 is heavier in the head than one with the same grip and shaft that weighs C-8; D-0 is heavier than C-9; D-1 is heavier than D-0; D-2 is heavier than D-1; and so on. Swingweight in itself isn't as important as overall weight or deadweight, in my opinion, but it does give manufacturers a way of seeing that every club in a given set has more or less the same *distribution* of weighting, so that each club feels more or less like the others when swung.

BUYING CLUBS

It should be obvious by now that a lot goes into properly fitting a golfer with a set of clubs. The clubs that I endorse are sold through retail stores, as opposed to pro shops, but I still advise any serious golfer to work with a pro when it comes to buying a set that will be personalized to his or her needs. The clubs you buy from a pro will be more expensive, but if you want the best fitting, that's the route you should go.

If you are a beginner and unsure whether or not you'll like the game, I suggest you buy a set of less expensive clubs from a retail store or a secondhand set from a pro shop. This set might not fit you perfectly, but it will do the job until you find out if you want to stick with golf. Actually, a good set of clubs that's, say, two years old probably won't cost too much, since depreciation will already have reduced the price. You could probably use that set for a year or so and then get your money back on a trade-in deal for a new set.

If you do buy a new set of clubs, I strongly suggest that it include a 5 wood or a 6 wood, instead of a 2 wood. You'll find that these clubs, with their extra loft, will serve you well on shots from rough and on long approaches to the green where you need more height than you'd normally get with a 2 iron or 3 iron. Only the very best players can use a 2 wood from the fairway and still get the ball high into the air. I personally feel that a driver, a 3 wood, and a 5 wood would be about the only woods you'd ever really need. The 4 wood would be a luxury for most golfers.

If you happen to be a parent of a youngster starting golf, please don't turn your old clubs over to him without modifying them first. I've seen more young people's golf swings ruined with adult clubs than you can imagine. Juniors simply can't handle clubs of adult length and weight. If they try to do so, they'll build some bad habits into their swings that it can take a lifetime—and then some—to eliminate.

Instead, ask the pro to cut down your clubs' length before you give them to Junior to use. When he gets bigger and stronger you can always bring the same clubs back to standard length by merely removing the grips and sticking extension plugs into the ends of the handles.

THE FINAL WORD

MY MAIN PURPOSE in writing this book has been to save you from embarrassing yourself on the golf course. I hope that you'll work hard on the things I've suggested, and that you'll have enough success so that you can play without fear of making yourself look too foolish.

There will be times when things won't go as you'd hoped they would. At such times you may feel embarrassed, just as I have on countless occasions out on tour. But don't let that throw you. Keep working on your game. The more you practice and play, the less embarrassment you'll suffer. When you do make a mistake, don't fret about it. Chances are that someone over in a nearby fairway is making an even bigger mess of things. And certainly those you'll be playing with will have had their share of embarrassment.

What I'm really saying is that I hope you'll remember that golf is a game, and games are supposed to be fun.

Thanks for taking the time to read my book. I hope you'll feel free to discuss it with me if our paths should ever cross down the road.